The Power of Half

To Bin Bin,

Find your passion!

[signature]

KEVIN SALWEN & HANNAH SALWEN

The Power *of* Half

One Family's Decision
to Stop Taking
and Start Giving Back

HOUGHTON MIFFLIN HARCOURT
Boston – New York – 2010

For information about permission to reproduce
selections from this book, write to Permissions,
Houghton Mifflin Harcourt Publishing Company,
215 Park Avenue South, New York, New York 10003.

www.hmhbooks.com

Library of Congress Cataloging-in-Publication Data
Salwen, Kevin.
The power of half : one family's decision to stop taking
and start giving back / Kevin Salwen and Hannah Salwen.
   p. cm.
 ISBN 978-0-547-24806-6
   1. Consumption (Economics)—Moral and ethical aspects—
United States. 2. Consumer behavior—Moral and ethical
aspects—United States. I. Salwen, Hannah. II. Title.
   HC110.C6S255 2009
   174—dc22   2009029971

Book design by Melissa Lotfy

Printed in the United States of America

DOC 10 9 8 7 6 5 4 3 2 1

For Joan and Joseph,
our teammates through this journey
and all others

Contents

Contents

Introduction

O UR FAMILY IS a fairly typical Atlanta foursome: two baby boomers (Joan and Kevin) and two teenagers (Hannah and Joseph). Our days consist of the standard American life—school, work, and youth sports. For more than a decade we aspired to the usual "stuff": new cars, a spacious home, nice vacations. Sure, we took on the occasional volunteer activity, feeding the homeless and building Habitat for Humanity houses, but largely we were consumed by our careers and enhancing our lifestyle through bigger, newer, better. We were focused on us.

We moved into a huge "Dream House," large enough for us to scatter in different directions. As we drove from activity to activity, the TV in the back seat kept the kids entertained—and our family from connecting. At dinner, conversations began to center on to-do lists instead of meaningful dialogue. Our sense of togetherness was beginning to erode. I can't pinpoint the moment it happened because, after all, erosion is so much harder to recognize than earthquake damage. Still, when we stopped to take a hard look, it was clear that we were drifting apart. We were losing our core.

Then our life took an amazing turn.

Prodded by Hannah, who at fourteen had become increasingly upset about the imbalance of opportunities in the world, we launched an audacious family project. We decided to sell our 6,500-square-foot landmark home, move to a nondescript house that was half as big, and donate half of the sales price to help alleviate poverty in one of the neediest corners of the planet. We committed to donating more than $800,000 for work in two dozen villages in Ghana— a place we not only hadn't visited, but one so foreign to us that we had to look it up on the map.

The result was a remarkable family adventure. Around our dinner table, we spent hours discussing the world's problems and how we might help. We made every decision in our two-year journey collectively, with kids having just as much say as parents.

But this book is more than just the tale of a family trying to turn the good life into a life of good. It's about unintended consequences, like the way inventors stumbled across penicillin or Post-it notes or Flubber. Yes, we're helping the world a bit. But in the process we are transforming our relationships with one another. And that has been the real surprise.

During this adventure, Hannah and Joseph became empowered and confident, which enabled them to relate much more deeply to each other and to Joan and me. Our family discussions became more democratic, more open, more honest. By sharing decision-making, Joan and I became better at listening to the other members of our family. Several times Hannah said to me, "My friends never discuss things with their parents," and then told me what she was thinking about people or events.

We have learned to converse about big human issues, and while we're talking, we often veer into a discussion about other things we wouldn't previously have shared, like adolescent relationships or even sex or drugs. Don't get me wrong—our family isn't perfect (far from it), but we have found a broader avenue for communication. And I'm willing to bet that many families would be glad to have that.

So, Cool Thing #1 is that the old maxim "the more you give, the more you get" is actually true. Setting out to be selfless became the most self-interested thing we ever did. We truly brought our family together.

Then there is Cool Thing #2: just about everything we've done can be replicated, regardless of the economy or individual asset level. *The Power of Half* is more about *how* we undertook our family project than about what we did. Some people say to us, "I could never sell my house." Who expects you to? Our project was never about size. We chose to sell our house because it was something that our family could handle from the perspective of giving half. But as you'll learn in this book, your "half" can be whatever you choose, at whatever budget you set.

Why half? Because it's measurable. Often when caring individuals see social problems, our gut reaction is "I ought to do more." But "more" is too vague to be useful, and we usually end up not doing much of anything. By contrast, "half" provides a metric to live with, a way to set a standard to push us to achieve.

You can be creative—a little goes a long way. To offer a simple example: if your family watches four hours of television a week, you could jointly decide to halve that, then choose as a family to devote those extra two hours to some unified purpose. Care about the elderly? You might work together in a nursing home. AIDS patients? Maybe serve meals once a week for those two hours.

Cool Thing #3 is that *The Power of Half* not only works for so-called intact families but also provides great opportunities to connect divorced families, nontraditional families, and intergenerational ones.

No matter what your family makeup is, no matter what your version of "half" is, the secret is the process. Steal it, then use it to build your relationships. In an era of iPods, video games, headphones, and other isolating technology, *The Power of Half* can help you create your own connected journey. As the French essayist Michel de Montaigne said, "He who does not live in some degree for others, hardly lives for himself."

The Power of Half

1

The Treadmill

— — — - — - — - -

Unless someone like you cares a whole awful lot,
nothing is going to get better. It's not.

— Dr. Seuss, *The Lorax*

It's flat-out awkward for two people to share a pair of sewing scissors among their ten right-hand fingers, but Hannah and the tribal chief are trying their best. After a few seconds of what looks like thumb wrestling, they evenly control the scissors' gray plastic handle, then carefully move toward the sky-blue ribbon stretched across the door in front of them.

Forget Oscar Madison and Felix Unger. This is the oddest couple I've ever seen: a grinning fifteen-year-old white American girl in her wicking REI khakis and an earnest seventyish African tribal chief in gold and brown ceremonial robes worn like a toga across his left shoulder. She speaks English and has come six thousand miles for this. He speaks the tribal language Twi, and I'm guessing he has never left the West African nation of Ghana, except for maybe a vacation journey to neighboring Togo or Burkina Faso.

1

Yet here they are, pairing up for the opening ceremony of this new hand-cranked corn mill. For all their differences, they share a goal of helping this rural community on its path out of poverty, the chief because these are his people and Hannah because she is so eager to make the world a little better that she has uprooted her family and pledged more than $800,000 to help villagers in a country she couldn't locate on a map a year ago.

Their eyes meet for a second, the chief's gray goatee and mostly bald head contrasting with Hannah's auburn hair, which falls to the middle of her back and is frizzing in the July West African heat. The chief is silent as Hannah quickly and quietly counts, "One, two, three." Her plan is for them to squeeze the scissors at precisely the same time. As usual, Hannah is striving for fairness.

I am standing on the other side of the ribbon, swelling with pride in our daughter. For months we've been talking about moments just like this: How doing with a little less ourselves can improve the lives of people surviving on less than a dollar a day. How we can enable opportunity for African girls who otherwise would carry corn for hours, missing school while their parents work in the fields. How humble structures like this simple cinder-block building will keep more young women pursuing education, creating much better life options for themselves. Now that dream is happening right before my eyes. And Hannah, the girl who so often crawled into bed with my wife, Joan, and me when she was younger, is fully in charge, almost an adult in her own right.

· · ·

Only an hour ago our family had arrived here in Abisu Number One, which we were thrilled to find on our very detailed, two-sided map of Ghana. Amazingly, in a country no bigger than the state of Oregon, we have spent two days visiting village after village too insignificant to be mapped. That said, Abisu Number One doesn't even get its own name, instead sharing it with nearby Abisu Number Two.

But that's part of why this mill is such a big deal. If your community is too insignificant to merit its own name, you're not going to have the political muscle to get any resources. Forget rising to the top of the list for the food processor, school project, or health-care facility. In Abisu Number One's case, it hasn't received electricity or running water either.

As we emerged from our vehicles in Abisu Number One, Hannah, her brother, Joseph, Joan, and I might as well have been wearing neon arrows screaming *"Look here!"* Like it or not, we are the center of attention. *We* are the outsiders—not just people from somewhere else, but the most foreign people for miles, miles uncrossed by villagers who don't have transportation. Small children point. They call us *obruni* (white person) as they see what they've never seen before, people with pale skin. They want to touch us, shake our hands, feel our arms, understand whether we're different.

For our teenagers, it's a new world being the "other." For all of Hannah's and Joseph's lives, they have been the majority: white kids in a mostly white world, English-speakers in an English-language society, affluent in an affluent community. Now we are the different ones, the ones with the name that the majority calls us.

"It was really awkward to be put in the spotlight and kind of frightening at first to be the odd one out," Joseph told me later. "It gave me kind of a fish-out-of-water experience." Our five-foot, ten-inch redhead was about to turn fourteen, so there was no shortage of awkwardness in his life, but it was impossible to deny how much he stood out as the white kid with braces (a dental procedure, coincidentally, that cost as much as this corn mill we're dedicating, about $6,000).

Hannah and the chief are poised at the ribbon, and she has reached the count of three. Snip, cheer, and the race is on.

Scores of cheering villagers sprint through the cut ribbon to the building's front door and pass under the hand-painted sign that announces the grandly and awkwardly named Improved Food Production and Security Program Food Processor. They are eager to see the mill, which will grind the corn used to make kenkey, a sticky, polenta-like food that serves as the staple for each day's meals.

I don't realize it, but Joan doesn't race in with me. Always the reflective one in our family, she pauses to ponder the ribbon now dangling outside the building's front door. Hannah and the chief had cut the strip almost perfectly in half. *Half,* Joan was thinking. *How appropriate.*

Inside the mill, a villager attaches the crank to the machine, which looks like a large supermarket meat grinder. One turn, a second turn, then the mill whirs to life. A cheer reverberates off the peach cinder-block walls and corrugated metal roof. Jubilant men and women grab handfuls of corn and toss them into the intake bin; others grab the powdery meal coming out the bottom and fling it into the air.

"The energy in the room was amazing," Hannah later wrote in her diary. "I'd never seen people so happy, and especially for grain! Unbelievable."

Not surprisingly, this moment had quite an impact on our fifteen-year-old. As Hannah told me later, "I couldn't believe that something taken completely for granted in our society could mean so much in another. We don't even realize the measures that these people go through to make huge changes in their community that seem insignificant in ours."

She gets it! Is it parenting? Or are Joan and I finally catching up to what Hannah has long known—that our little band of four has the power to make a difference?

We're a long way from home in every way. It's not just that Ghana is across the Atlantic Ocean from where we live in Atlanta, Georgia. It's more a frame of mind.

I'll explain. I grew up in Brooklyn, the youngest of three children and the only boy in our Jewish family. My parents, as the expression goes, put the *dys* in *dysfunctional,* bitterly battling for years until they split for good when I was fourteen. My solution to all this was simple: just disappear. As I was graduating from high school, I figured a thousand miles was about far enough to leave the set of the real family feud behind. So I headed to Northwestern University, outside Chicago.

When I think back, charity was nowhere on my family's radar. I can't remember a single day of volunteering anywhere. I can't remember making any contributions, except the day in the 1960s when my family gave away an old winter coat to "a bum" (the common term back then) on the Bowery in lower Manhattan. For my mother, a desire to hold on to what she had wasn't surprising; having grown up as the daughter of an immigrant elevator operator and a piecework seamstress, she never felt comfortable giving anything away, even as she advanced to become a college professor.

My dad, the proverbial angry young man who aged into an angry old man, wasn't about to do the government's work. A lifelong socialist, he told me more than once, "There should be no need for charity. The government should take care of people's needs. Period."

At Northwestern, Joan King was three years behind me, a freshman when I was a senior. She was unlike anyone I had ever met. Joan had grown up in the most stable, most normal, most Protestant household I could imagine. She was completely unethnic. Her grandparents weren't just American-born; the family had generations of history tilling the rich black soil of Iowa.

Joan's family perceived charity the way many middle-class Americans did in the '60s and '70s: take care of the family first, then the church. There was the UNICEF box at Halloween, the occasional project with the Boy Scouts. But in general the United Methodist Church's mission arm, UMCOR, would handle the good works with the family's contributions.

Behind our clearly different upbringings, Joan and I recognized kindred spirits. The kids of four teachers, we knew the value of education. And we were eager to build careers, snare promotions, upgrade our lifestyle.

After graduation I joined the *Wall Street Journal,* where I moved from entry-level copy editor to reporter to columnist, then to the Washington bureau to help cover the first Bush administration and then the Clinton administration. I flew on Air Force One, interviewed senators on the private Capitol subway, did the black-tie party scene with those unnamed "senior administration officials." Meanwhile, Joan was hired by the consulting firm that would become Accenture. There, through an intense work ethic and a good eye for smart mentors, Joan systematically knocked down the dominoes of projects and promotions as part of that second generation of successful businesswomen that came just after the trailblazers. She helped the state of Washington build a better tax system and New York City's Board of Elections become more efficient.

Almost imperceptibly we rushed into our Accumulation Years. You know them, don't you? You earn more, you live larger. The bigger house, the more spacious apartment. Then, of course, the stuff to adorn that growing space. There were nicer vacations—travel to Alaska, Bermuda, Italy. We bought our first pieces of original art, cashmere sweaters at Christmas. Spending money meant having fun; buying electronic equipment or jewelry for each other was a token of love.

During recessions we thought twice about how to spend, but those were mere pauses on the upward trajectory. The goal was always to upgrade.

On Labor Day in 1992, five years into our marriage, bald

little Hannah was born at George Washington University Hospital in D.C. The teacher and writer Elizabeth Stone once called having a child a decision to "have your heart go walking outside your body." At Hannah's birth, Joan burst into tears. As she said, "It was not until I looked into my daughter's little eyes that I realized how much my own mother loved me." We quickly read a bunch of parenting books—Benjamin Spock, Penelope Leach, *What to Expect in the First Year*—looking for any information to make us better nurturers of this blob of protoplasm.

But as our hearts expanded, so did our spending. The car got larger: a nice Volvo replaced the Honda Accord. Our travel didn't stop either; we just took Hannah, who traveled to London and Paris on Joan's business trips before she was two. In her first passport photo, we had to prop Hannah up in her Hanna Andersson outfit to keep her from falling over.

The funny thing is, we never even thought much about our spending, especially once we started having kids. Who could skimp on them? Ours might have been an extreme case, but I'll bet you've had those moments, too, hurtling without much thought from one purchase to the next. A jacket, a better TV, new furniture for the kid's room—hey, isn't that why God created credit cards? For us, accumulation was just part of the job description, particularly during the economic good times.

We weren't *trying* to be obnoxious, consuming yuppies, we just were. This was the American Dream, wasn't it, to live better than your parents did? We were lucky to have everything we had, not because of inheritance or lottery but through a confluence of hard work, career dedication, and being in the right place at the right time. For instance, our comfort with spending grew in 1993 when Joan made partner at Accenture and our disposable income jumped again. To celebrate, I threw her a champagne-tasting party at our Washington townhouse.

The next year, 1994, we moved to Atlanta, and soon after came the even bigger move to the Dream House. With three full floors, 116 Peachtree Circle was one of Atlanta's gorgeous historic homes. Nearly one hundred years old, with soaring Corinthian columns, the house had originally been the home of the aptly named Rich family, builders of Atlanta's most successful homegrown department stores. Now we were movin' on up. This would be the perfect place to hold big parties and host events.

Joseph came along in 1994, and our family was complete. Two redheaded children with fair complexions, Hannah and Joseph were a perfect blend of Joan and me, with features that drew more from the Salwen side, coloring that honored the Kings.

Hannah and Joseph grew up with very different social personalities. Hannah always demanded to be with others. When she was about seven, she began to harbor fears that people close to her might die at any time, so when any of us left her, whether on a run to Kroger for milk, on a three-day business trip, or at the end of a phone call, she would close the conversation with a perky "Love you." If the end came, "Love you" would be the last thing you'd heard from Hannah. Maybe a dozen times a day.

Joseph, in contrast, was so comfortable with himself that he rarely noticed when others left the room. But he loved to amuse people. One year for Halloween he decided to be a movie-theater carpet. We found a remnant piece of broadloom and cut a head hole in it, and he decorated it with chewed-up bubble gum, smooshed Milk Duds, glued-on popcorn, and torn tickets. Later that night, when he trick-or-treated, Joseph refused to tell people what he was, offering only a taunting little "Guess" when they asked. Probably 90 percent figured it out, which filled him with pride; he loved the game.

At times of disagreement, our family style was to confront issues head on. Years earlier Joan had brought into our marriage a "no sleeping until the argument is finished" rule; as a result, she and I resolved debates sometimes long into the night, but resolved they were.

We brought that into our parenting too. When Hannah was nine, a fear of dogs that had been percolating grew into a full-blown phobia. The first question she would ask when invited for a play date was a tension-filled "Do they have dogs?" We tried to reason with her, take her to friends who had calm pets, read her more books about animals. But Hannah's fear didn't subside. In the end, in Joan's typical "resolve the issue" fashion, we headed for the Humane Society to adopt a dog and brought home a border collie–ish mix named Maggie, who Hannah apprehensively decided was calm enough to deal with.

The girl and the dog formed a fragile truce. The first few days after we adopted Maggie, Hannah insisted that they remain on opposite sides of a closed door; when the dog came into the kitchen, Hannah perched on the counter, far from the potential licking and sniffing. But over the weeks and months, Hannah's fear of dogs subsided. She fed Maggie, and briefly petted her. As important, she began to visit pet-owning friends. Crisis averted.

It would have been difficult to differentiate us from other families. Two parents, two kids, nice house, dog. We worked hard, got our promotions, came home. There we pitched baseballs to Hannah and Joseph, did art projects, read books. Shopping for stuff expanded beyond buying what Joan and I desired to include what the kids "needed," creating plenty of new opportunities for accumulation: batting and pitching instruction, acting camps, music lessons, travel teams. Like others we knew, we bought most things we wanted.

Don't get me wrong: money is not a bad thing. Far from it. But spend, spend, spend becomes a brutal way to raise kids; they start to believe that everything is replaceable or that everything costs the same amount. An ever-escalating standard of living becomes the New Normal, something they grow accustomed to.

When our kids were old enough to start school, we sent them to the Westminster Schools, one of Atlanta's elite private institutions. Boasting thirteen academic buildings and nine athletic fields on 180 acres in affluent Buckhead, Westminster feels like a lovely college campus. Lexuses, Mercedes, and Lincolns idle in the carpool lanes as mothers wait in their tennis clothes, motors running to keep their BlackBerries charged and themselves comfortably air-conditioned.

You know the classic analogy: the devil appears on one shoulder, urging you to follow your base instincts; the angel on the other shoulder prods you to pass up temptation and keep your conscience clear. In our case, the devil urged us to buy more stuff as the angel prodded us to stop the madness and instill better values in our kids. In the carpool lane, the shoulder devil offered a steady stream of advice: Check out that Hummer. Join the private golf club. Ski at Beaver Creek. Look what those people have! I could almost hear the angel groan in disgust.

One Thursday when Joseph was in the third grade, we encountered a laughable new level. He had been invited to his buddy Thomas's grandfather's south Georgia "farm," a former plantation where quail hunting was the centerpiece. Farm? Nothing like what Joan knew from her grandparents in Iowa, that's for sure. The day before the mother was to drive Joseph the three hours south, our phone rang. "Kevin, would you mind if we rode in my father's private plane down there? Dad is flying down there anyway, so we thought we'd hitch a ride with him." While it was gracious of the mother to double-check with us, the cold, hard truth was this: Joseph was now jetting to play dates.

The British economist and businessman Charles Handy writes about keeping up with the Joneses in his book *The Elephant and the Flea:* "Life becomes a long-distance race that you cannot afford to quit, but also one that you can never win, because there is always someone ahead, always more to get." Joan and I simply called it "the treadmill." We created a lifestyle; then, just to keep up, we had to stay in motion. And like the automated treadmill, it had a built-in mechanism to keep it going. We'd never dream of going from power windows back to hand-cranked ones or leather seats to cloth. In fact, I couldn't remember any time we had done that in any facet of our lives—cars, houses, electronics, or musical instruments. Better, nicer, more became the New Normal.

All this comes with a cost, of course, and I'm not talking about the obvious financial price tag. Think about having to keep trading up professionally, fighting for that promotion or battling for that raise. The treadmill demands it. At Joan's firm, it was even baked into the system: under the "up or out" structure, anyone who didn't earn more partnership units switched from the fast track to an encouraged departure. It's easy to view just about everything through a financial prism, rationalizing along the way. ("What if I take this promotion three hundred miles away and see my family on weekends? It's only two years, and I can make fifteen thousand dollars more.")

I love the perspective of my friend Mark Albion, a former Harvard Business School professor who helps people improve themselves and the world through responsible business. (Mark and I have talked often about parenting and debated the question, "Are we raising consumers or citizens?") For Mark, the battle to keep up with the Joneses can be translated into drug terms. "Success, power, money, and fame have the undoubted strength of the best of narcotics: they create a deep silence," he explains in his newsletter, *Making a Life, Making a Living.* "It is certain that the material offers security. At least, for a while."

But as with narcotics, this high is a path to nowhere. Consider this: research shows that nearly four times as many people who make over $75,000 a year feel that they need at least 50 percent more income to meet their needs as those making less than $30,000. Mark's conclusion? "Trading our life energy for it, we often forget the real cost of money."

Looking back, I'm not sure Joan and I actually *forgot* the real cost of money. We never knew it, never gave it a thought. We were on autopilot in our careers and personal lives.

In turn, consumerism began to affect Hannah and Joseph, whose New Normal was a disposable, trade-up society. When Joseph was twelve, his Little League Baseball All-Star team was on a roll, winning the district championship. They had won the Georgia state championship as eleven-year-olds and now had a chance to go back-to-back. But as his team moved into the state tourney, the boys had a problem: the Anderson Techzilla bats that many of our guys, including Joseph, had been swinging were often denting, so that the umpires removed them from games.

We could have used one of the other bats in the basement, which were older but perfectly good. But they weren't Techzillas, and our culture dictated that we provide the "best" for our kids. And our kids expected the "best." No adjustment required. So one of the other dads on the team searched local distributors and bought five new bats at two hundred dollars each. Joseph's team promptly lost in the state finals. Season over, bats in the basement.

Who can blame kids? Of course they will emulate their parents' consumer behavior. (Feel bad, buy something!) Beyond that, by some estimates, kids are bombarded with as many as five thousand ad impressions each day, on billboards, TV, T-shirts, and anywhere else you can think of. "Our culture is working overtime to addict young people to spending, and the message is always this: if you just had one more thing, you'd be happy," notes Nathan Dungan, the creator of Share Save Spend, a Minneapolis-based company that helps parents teach kids about financial responsibility.

I should make clear at this point that the angel on the shoulder was trying to fight back. Even as we had ramped up spending in our marriage, Joan and I had worked in the community, tutoring young readers and serving senior citizens. After Hannah was born, Joan took her along on deliveries of Meals on Wheels. Often the octogenarians ignored their box lunches but paused to hug the toddler in her Gap Kids outfits.

As we focused on our careers, Joan and I often took on service work for professional reasons. She ran her firm's United Way campaign, a nice visible assignment, and became the chairperson of Accenture's local foundation. She joined the Alexis de Tocqueville Society, a United Way group for annual givers of $10,000 or more. It was philanthropy as business mission.

Occasionally we would hunt for ways to involve our kids. For instance, when we began working on Habitat for Humanity houses, Joan and I would drag Hannah and Joseph to the dedications on the final Saturday. There they often found that the home-buyers had children their age. Joseph sometimes took a ball and played with the kids on the street, and afterward, on the drive home, we'd talk about similarities and differences. And like a lot of families, we used the rule of thirds for our kids' weekly allowance, requiring that equal parts be dropped into canisters for spending, saving, and giving to charity.

In short, we did more than many families, trying to find our center. But we were still a long way from being able to answer some really critical questions: What did our family stand for? What did we want to be—not do or have, but *be*? Now that I think of it, we didn't even ask those questions.

In fact, we were running so fast on the treadmill, we almost missed a huge clue. Amid the frenzy of a family life filled with work and kids' activities, an emotional storm was brewing within Hannah, and it nearly escaped Joan's and my notice.

At Westminster, the kids were part of the school's growing curriculum on service and philanthropy. The school had just created a program called Urban Edventure, in which the ninety or so students in Hannah's fifth grade volunteered for two days instead of attending classes, with a sleepover where they watched the movie *Pay It Forward*. The first day, Hannah worked at a downtown Atlanta restaurant and service program called Café 458. We would look back on that day as a true milestone.

Set in a two-story brick building near the King Center, Café 458 serves a gourmet brunch on weekends. It's not unusual to find Carolina pulled-pork eggs Benedict or Grand Marnier French toast on the Sunday menu. But the twist is that all the profit, even the tips for the volunteer servers, goes to fund a program that helps homeless men and women get back on a path to success. Most important for Hannah, there is a weekday meal program for the homeless in the same restaurant.

Café 458 was the pilot light for Hannah's fuel. After working during Urban Edventure, she came home full of life, reciting at dinner a quote from former congresswoman Shirley Chisholm that hung on the café wall: "Service is the rent we pay for the privilege of living on this earth." She asked if she could volunteer there again—not exactly an offer even a semiclueless parent could refuse. So once a week for several months the eleven-year-old Hannah prepared food and served lunch to homeless Atlantans trying to get their lives on track.

Now, instead of talking about friends or her teachers, many days Hannah came home bubbling with stories about the homeless people she had served at the café, especially Henry, a lonely man who always sat alone. "It's so sad, Dad. Nobody likes him, and he always sits at a table by himself," she said. That, of course, just made Hannah want to stop by Henry's table even more frequently, offering him refills of water or iced tea from the clear plastic pitchers.

Looking back, Joan and I had undergone significant changes in our own focus on service, the most obvious being the career shifts we had made just a couple of years earlier. At Accenture, Joan had run the firm's national women's mentoring task force, helping younger women move through the promotion pipeline. But now, after twenty years at the firm, she recognized a serious problem. "It drives me nuts," Joan told me. "Too many of the thirtysomething women have never learned to enjoy taking risks or to advocate for themselves." Her solution: she needed to reach women earlier—in other words, to teach school.

She sprang the concept on me during a walk around our

leafy neighborhood in the fall of 2001. Her proposal was jarring, of course; it's hard to see a 95 percent pay cut as anything but. Sure, we had stock from an Accenture IPO, but the vagaries of the stock market were a tricky thing to rely on.

As we walked together along the oak-lined streets, Joan posed the million-dollar question (literally): "What if we run out of money?" My reaction was so quick it was almost thoughtless. After all, just a year earlier I'd had my own career shift, leaving the comfort of the *Wall Street Journal* after eighteen years to co-create a magazine company. I wasn't going to shoot her dream down, money or no money. I reminded her of our first apartment in New York, a one-bedroom measuring less than 700 square feet (or about one ninth of the Dream House). "We've lived with a lot less before," I said. "I guess we would just do it again."

So Joan earned a master's degree and soon signed on to teach seventh-grade English at the Atlanta Girls' School. Now she would have the opportunity to prepare girls to be more successful women.

Because of our job changes, Joan and I began to spend more time at home with the kids. But nothing about those career moves and our growing kids made things simpler. Whose lives are, anyhow? If there is anything that parents complain about more than anything else, it's busyness. But sadly, busy becomes the excuse for not doing the things that truly matter. The funny thing is, we all know that we're overbooked, too busy for quality time.

Each element of busy has a rationale. Our kids loved sports, and of course we couldn't skimp there, so we rushed them to lessons, camps, and teams. We were helping our kids; who couldn't justify that? Like lots of families, we figured we could make it up on vacations, trying to squeeze love and togetherness into a few weeks a year.

But we were losing our core. As Hannah and Joseph grew older and more independent, they naturally entered their own orbits, with Joan and me increasingly transforming into chauffeurs. Weekend trips to Lenox Mall were aimed at socializing with friends, movies became parent-free affairs, iPods blared in ears, DVDs provided the entertainment on car trips. Conversation rarely reached any significant depth. Our family was spinning into different galaxies.

Still, there were glimmers of hope. Through it all, the one constant was dinner, and come hell or high water we would eat together. Many nights we'd wait for Joseph to finish baseball practice and eat at eight. Or we'd throw him into the car, drive to where Hannah had a volleyball match in the northern suburbs, cheer her on, and grab pizza afterward. It might only be a twenty-minute gathering, but it was the centering event of our family day.

And there were the stories. From the time the kids were little, I loved sharing pieces from the newspaper or radio. Sometimes it was an article about new words being added to the dictionary. Other times it was a great inspiring tale. Hannah even picked up on the idea, reading aloud her favorite *Chicken Soup for the Soul* stories at the table. One story would lead to another; the more sappy and inspirational, the better.

One night at dinner I recalled a story from National Public Radio about the robbery at knifepoint of a New Yorker. The victim, Julio Diaz, described it like this:

> He wants my money, so I just gave him my wallet and told him, "Here you go." As the teen began to walk away, Diaz told him, "Hey, wait a minute. You forgot something. If you're going to be robbing people for the rest of the night, you might as well take my coat to keep you warm."
>
> The robber looked at his would-be victim, "like what's going on here?" Diaz says. "He asked me, 'Why are you doing this?'"
>
> Diaz replied: "If you're willing to risk your freedom for a few dollars, then I guess you must really need the money. I mean, all I wanted to do was get dinner and if you really want to join me . . . hey, you're more than welcome."

The teenager joined Diaz for the meal, and, after they ate, Diaz asked him for the knife, which the young man gave him. The piece concluded with Diaz saying, "I figure, you know, if you treat people right, you can only hope that they treat you right. It's as simple as it gets in this complicated world."

When I finished, Joseph was silent, digesting the story. Hannah gasped: "Oh, that is amazing. It's so cool."

I looked over at Joan, and I knew what she was thinking. Our minds were spinning with possibilities. The career changes. The volunteering. Hannah's enthusiasm. *Maybe we're not hopeless, just on the wrong track.*

Joan and I didn't know it at the time, but our teenaged girl would be the driver of that new train.

HANNAH'S TAKE

Believing You Can Make a Difference

ABOUT 111 WOMEN DIE OF BREAST CANCER EVERY DAY IN THE United States. A million teenagers get pregnant each year. Someone dies every thirty-one minutes because of drunken drivers. I'm not writing this to bum you out. But you might be thinking, *There are so many problems, there's no way that I or any one person could solve anything.*

When civil-rights activist Rosa Parks refused to move to the back of a public bus in 1955, she never dreamed of the impact she would have on millions of lives. "I didn't have any idea just what my actions would bring about," she said years later. "At the time I was arrested I didn't know how the community would react." The reason Ms. Parks didn't get up is that she knew the racist laws were wrong.

Rosa Parks is just one of the thousands of influential people whose actions changed the views of many people today. Think about Gandhi, Mother Teresa, Greg Mortenson, John Woolman, Madame Curie (if you don't know them, check them out; they're all remarkable). Sometimes small acts significantly affect a large group of people. But even when they don't, they can have a big influence, maybe on just one individual.

So don't get discouraged because you can't solve a whole problem alone. As the British philosopher Edmund Burke said, "Nobody made a greater mistake than he who did nothing because he could only do a little." I know exactly what he was talking about. Before our family project I kept telling myself that no matter how hard I tried or how much money I gave, I would never be able to fully solve any of the world's big problems. When I worked at Café 458, the Atlanta restaurant for homeless men and women, I saw dozens of people come in looking depressed and lonely. But still I didn't see them as individuals, but instead as a group, "the homeless."

Then one day at Café 458 I heard two homeless men talking about a college basketball game that I had watched with my dad the night before. I snapped to the realization that these people are people. How stupid and rude I had been to see them as different from me. I realize now that having that epiphany was a big step for me. In that split second of comprehension, I switched from seeing them as a group of people to viewing them as individuals. When I started seeing people in need as individuals, the problem of homelessness and hunger seemed smaller and I felt like I could make more of a difference. I also started believing that I could help because the problem was on a personal level.

Activity

Think of a person from your community who inspires you. Look beyond his or her specific actions to the kind of qualities that person brings to work or volunteer activities. For example, some people are better at creating new programs than at actually putting them into action; other people are doers, ready to take someone else's ideas and run with them. Is that aunt in your family a problem-solver? A good listener? An inspirer?

Now think about your strengths in the same light. If you took your best characteristics out into the world, how could you use them to make a difference? Are you patient? Maybe you would be a good tutor. Are you musical? Maybe you could be playing the guitar at a nursing home (and bringing your family along to sing — no talent required). We all have gifts the world can use.

2

You Don't Know Till You Listen

— — — - — - — -

The purpose of life is . . . above all to matter, to count,
to stand for something, to have it make some difference
that we lived at all.

—Leo Rosten

HANNAH AND I were driving along the Buford Highway Connector in our silver Scion—the Toaster, we call it, because of its boxy shape— headed home from one of Hannah's sleepovers with a school friend. The Connector starts as a highway off-ramp from Interstate 85, then slows to a city street, with a stoplight marking the transition at Spring Street. It might be the hardest light in all of Atlanta to make, since the Spring Street traffic has the green light at least three times as long as the Connector traffic does.

Because cars have to stop there for a long time, the Connector-Spring corner has become a popular spot for homeless men and women to ask for money. Where drivers must wait, there is solicitation opportunity. For us, this spot has often been a place where we hand out the five-dollar Mc-

Donald's Arch cards we carry in the glove compartment; distributing cards makes us more confident that the recipients will buy food, not booze or drugs.

On this fall day in 2006, I rounded the curve to leave the Connector and slowed the car from 60 to zero as we pulled up to the red light, less than a mile from our house. Not surprisingly, sitting to our left, perched in front of a rusting chainlink fence, was a homeless man. We would never learn his name, and he would never know the enormous impact he would have on our family—or on the lives of thousands of others.

To me, there was nothing unusual about his look (he wore a ragged T-shirt and jeans), and certainly nothing innovative about his cardboard sign shakily hand-printed in black Sharpie: HUNGRY, HOMELESS, PLEASE HELP. I was consumed with my internal dialogue: *Damn, I'm out of McDonald's cards. Should I give him cash? No, just sit tight.* I squirmed in my seat, avoiding eye contact.

But over in the passenger seat, Hannah was having quite a different experience. As she looked at the homeless man, a sight she had seen dozens of times before, on this day his situation registered more deeply. That's because when she looked in the other direction, she spotted another man driving a black Mercedes coupe.

If Joseph had been riding with me, he and I might have discussed the Mercedes' convertible top or the owner's color choice. Not Hannah. Her head swiveled right and left between the Mercedes and the homeless man, processing the have and the have-not. She started talking slowly, thinking as she went. "Dad," she began, "if that man"—she pointed to the Mercedes—"had a less nice car, that man there"—she pointed to the homeless man—"could have a meal."

At some point or another, just about every mother or father says, "I wish there were an owner's manual for how to do this parenting thing." No doubt Joan and I have made a raft of kid-raising mistakes over the past decade and a half. But there is one crucial thing we've learned: teaching opportunities come unexpectedly and fleetingly. Pay attention; miss them and they're gone.

Sitting at that intersection, I began to realize that maybe I now had such an opportunity. I let Hannah's point hang there for a second, then answered: "Um, yeah. But you know, if *we* had a less nice car, he could have a meal." The light changed and we continued on our way home, but I knew we weren't finished talking about the world's disparities. As Hannah wrote months later in her journal, "Driving past the homeless man that one time changed my life. I felt sad, like I wanted to help him, but angry, really angry. At myself, mainly. Thinking there was so much I could do for this man, and for a lot of the poor people in this world considering I had so much."

When our foursome gathered for dinner, Hannah told Joan and Joseph what had happened. She described just how wrong it all felt, offering an exasperated "Dude, it sucks. We should fix this." The world was full of imbalance, we all acknowledged, but this time it was truly bugging Hannah.

In some ways it was a corollary to a philosophy Joan and I had tried to infuse into our family: Problems can be fixed. Our own. The world's. Don't whine about issues unless you have tried several solutions. We (and others) just have to work at it until we get the right answer. When I look back, I realize that our unspoken mantra was something like *Take action. Never accept things as they are when we have the chance to improve them.*

Hannah's observation was, of course, completely age-appropriate for a fourteen-year-old. After all, young people begin to notice the world around them more critically as they leave their childhood years, and they frequently dabble in activities that they think can help the world. They carry with them an idealized perspective—pretty nice, if you ask me. Experience may be a great teacher, but it also robs us of some of that "Why not?" spirit.

And Hannah was beginning to notice need all around. There had been her fifth-grade experiences at Café 458 with Henry and other homeless Atlantans, which she carried into the next year. Then, when she moved to the Atlanta Girls' School for seventh grade, her awareness ratcheted up to another level. Hannah is very much a visual learner, and two short films had energized her.

One night she had come home from school gushing about a video that a sophomore had created about genocide in Darfur. Sarah Hudson had become so outraged about the killings in Sudan that she had convinced the administration at Atlanta Girls' School to let her create Genocide Awareness Week. Posters covered the AGS walls, letters to senators urged intervention, an assembly highlighted the messages. But it was Sarah's movie that inspired Hannah the most. Hannah loaded it onto her computer and showed it to Joan before dinner, then insisted that all of us climb onto the king-size mattress in our master bedroom and watch the film together. To Hannah, the message was simple: speak up about big issues; act on the injustices you see.

A few months later Hannah's worldview expanded again as she fell in love with Sarah McLachlan's "World on Fire" music video. It opens with the singer sitting on a simple chair in a barren room on an otherwise empty set. A title card comes up: "What's wrong with this video? Well, it cost only $15." Then the song, featuring the lyrics "The more we take, the less we become / A fortune of one that means less for some," lists where the rest of the typical $150,000 cost of the film would have been spent ("a producer would cost $7,500"). The twist is that McLachlan's video dollars are used not on those typical production costs but to help poverty-stricken children and women in Cambodia, Niger, Bangladesh, India, and other struggling countries. (That would-be producer's salary instead bought "6 months of medicine for 5,000 patients" in a Nairobi health clinic.)

All told, Hannah must have watched the videos by the two Sarahs a combined thirty or forty times. (You can see Sarah McLachlan's at www.worldonfire.ca.)

These experiences added up to a single fairly obvious "Aha": there was no shortage of need in the world. Here at home, overseas, for children, women, animals, water, air, human rights, children's rights, orphans, AIDS, cancer, education, famine—the demand side was infinite.

On the supply side, it was becoming apparent to Joan and me that little about our family's charitable activities touched Hannah personally. She never saw the checks to charities we wrote at the end of each year. She knew our family worked at Habitat, the food bank, and the Central Night Shelter, but those activities weren't consistent enough and didn't really affect her.

So, on that autumn evening, Joan and I used Hannah's Mercedes incident at the Connector corner as an opportunity to educate the kids about the fact that we really were quite involved. Really. We told them about our annual giving. We reminded them of the volunteer work we did. "Remember that day playing bingo with the elderly people at Wesley Woods nursing home? That was good, right?" Joan said. "We know it's never enough, but it's a good place to start."

Even as the words came out, they sounded painfully lame; we were defensive about our family's contribution. And if those words sounded inadequate to us, in Hannah's mind our parental tutorial was even worse. It was pathetic. With each sentence of our defense, the question "So?" kept rattling around in her brain. Simply put, Joan and I just didn't get it.

Joseph, though, was doing just fine. For him the world was generally a happy-go-lucky place. Oh, he knew he had more than most, and he definitely understood that his role on this earth was to serve sometimes. But he was fully satisfied that we as a family were paying enough of a service tax, to echo Shirley Chisholm's words, and he wasn't about to prod us to do more.

Hannah didn't say much more that night, but it was clear as she and I loaded the dishwasher that she remained unconvinced of the seriousness of our family's contribution to society. Hannah's memory kept replaying those images of the homeless man and the Mercedes, wrestling with the disparity.

If there is a trait that Joan's gene pool dropped into Hannah's personality, it is tenacity. They both hate to lose, refuse to let go. There's an expression in our family, "Getting Joaned," which means that Joan relentlessly builds consensus for an audacious plan. Several years ago she Joaned some friends into buying a piece of North Georgia lake property from us through a ten-month-long, multi-conversation process. To them it was an evolutionary series of conversations, but Joan had thought it all through far in advance. A few years later she Joaned our kids into agreeing to a commerce-free Christmas of only homemade or handmade gifts. To be clear about this, there's nothing unethical about Joaning—our friends who bought the property would tell you that it was the best real estate investment they ever made. It's just a brilliantly orchestrated sequence that enables Joan to get what she wants.

We regarded Hannah as just a fledgling at the Joaning process, not yet able to do it as deftly as her mother could. But we underestimated her. Over the next few days our fourteen-year-old displayed a never-let-up spirit that was both startling and very hard to resist.

We saw Hannah's technique three days after the Mercedes/homeless man incident, when Joan called us into the breakfast room for Chinese takeout. Water glasses sat on our ribbed blue placemats, except for Joseph's, where a gallon jug of milk sat; he likes to chug straight from the container, so he gets his own milk, which he labels J in blue marker.

Joan, Joseph, and I shared the chicken and beef dishes. But, as usual, Hannah, the pickiest of eaters, had a different meal in front of her—on this night, fried rice with egg, no vegetables, no meat. Hannah doesn't eat meat, but it would be wrong to call her a vegetarian; she doesn't eat vegetables either. I guess she's a starchitarian.

From the moment we gathered at the table, it was clear that Hannah was in no mood for small talk. She had been stewing about our family's role in the world. Still dressed in her spandex volleyball shorts, ankle braces, and knee-pads from the practice of her school team, she didn't wait for conversation to develop or school talk to take over. The sequence went like this: Our family's usual blessing, offered as a group, with Joseph providing an extra ". . . and thank you for the dogs" at the end. A collective "Amen." The first bite. Then Hannah, not waiting even to swallow her fried rice, jolted us: "I really don't want to be the kind of family that just talks about doing things. I want to be a family that actually does them."

I was caught off-guard and mentally scrambled to put this in context—*Just talks about doing things? Family that actually does them?* Joan shot me a knowing look; the women clearly connected about this. But Joseph apparently was going through the same recall problem I was. "Hannah, what on earth are you talking about?" he asked.

"C'mon, Joe. Remember the homeless guy? Remember the Mercedes? I don't want to be a family that just sits around and says, 'I wish we could do something.' I want to get out there and really make a difference, even if it's a small difference."

Looking back at that moment, I realize that none of us should have been surprised by Hannah's spirit. After all, she was simply channeling the unspoken family narrative: *Never accept things as they are when we have the chance to improve them.*

A year or so earlier we had read as a family Paulo Coelho's book *The Alchemist,* the four of us propped up in Joan's and my bed, me reading aloud. (Who says you can't read aloud to your teenager?) Although the fable is a bit saccharine, *The Alchemist* introduced us to the concept of "personal legend." In other words, how did each of us want to be remembered—what was our real goal in life? Beyond a solo personal legend, though, we talked about whether there could be a family version of Coelho's concept, a collective legacy. Now, without the phrase "personal legend" entering into the conversation, that idea was spilling out from the soul of the girl in the volleyball kneepads who called her parents "dude."

The words came from Hannah's heart and eventually formed the cornerstone of our project (and our family). We would somehow have to become more than a family that just talks. We would have to become a family that does some of the hard work in the world. And we would need to do it together.

This time Joan was better prepared than she had been three days earlier. If Hannah was going to care this much about people she had never met, Joan wanted to see how much she was willing to sacrifice to change the lives of others. She had hinted to me that she might test Hannah. "What would happen if we challenged her to give up the things she owns, the items she really values?" Joan asked me. My mind immediately went to Hannah's clothes, stockpiled from plenty of mall trips. It didn't occur to me how bold the experiment would be, or how far it would stretch into all of our lives.

As Helen Keller once wrote, "Life is either a daring adventure—or it is nothing." So, when Hannah brought up the subject of doing more over dinner, Joan looked our daughter square in the eye. "What do you want to do," she said, "sell our house? Move into a smaller one and give what's left over to charity?"

Okay, I admit this was one hell of a test. What Joan had put on the table was this: Would we be willing to walk away from this gorgeous $2 million mansion, with its stunning Corinthian columns, spacious rooms, ample back yard, and, most important, decade's worth of our kids' memories? This home stood as a showplace, the kind of house that organizations sought out to have lavish parties in. We had hosted the kickoff of the Atlanta Habitat for Humanity capital campaign (I was on the board), the United Way Women's Initiative (Joan was on that board), the Atlanta Girls' School parents' fund. Neighborhood walkers often stopped to photograph the soaring façade, even without knowing that the house had history too: it had been the home of one of Atlanta's most fabled families. An elevator ran from the dining room to Hannah's gilded bedroom; it had been installed decades earlier, when the bedroom was a twenty-two-by-seventeen-foot dressing room.

For a teenager, there was no shortage of self-esteem wrapped up in having friends flock here for a Christmas party or for Halloween and marvel, "You live here?" "I have to admit, it was awesome having the cool house," Hannah told me later. "Two of my friends said that it looked like an art gallery. Or they'd say, 'You have a fireplace in your room? That's insane. *And* an elevator? Dude, whoa.'"

Cool house or not, increasingly it felt over the top, like an ill-fitting diamond necklace. It's a funny thing about collecting stuff that takes on its own inertia, a resistance to change. The need for bigger, nicer, more, becomes a force unto itself. Scientists define inertia as a force that keeps a body in motion moving in the same direction. Psychologists describe the situation as "an unconsciously chosen life script that narrows your choices"—in other words, being stuck. Either way, inertia/momentum/autopilot—call it what you like—is an incredibly powerful force to reverse.

But if that inertia breaks, doubt and questions creep in and change becomes something you can see or feel. We hadn't recognized it at the time, but the first crack in our momentum had come in an e-mail message Joan had received fifteen months earlier.

Here's what happened: The oak-floored, finished basement of our three-story house was a space we'd wrestled with for years. We wondered, *Should we build a media room? How about a game room? Music space?* Nothing felt right, so we left it essentially unused.

Then Hurricane Katrina hit, in August 2005. A few days after that shocking, deadly storm, Joan called me at work, breathless: "I want to talk to you seriously about something." She described how she had received one of those group e-mails that are easy to ignore. Then she read me the heart-wrenching description of a New Orleans–area family who needed a place to live in Atlanta. The mother, father, and two kids were living in their third shelter in six days, had lost their dog, and were now arriving in Atlanta with nowhere to sleep and no idea how long they might have to stay.

As we looked into the situation, the fit was about as perfect as could be. The family had a son, Duvey, around Joseph's age, and a four-year-old daughter, Eugenie. Even their last name, Salvant, seemed to scream good match for the Salwen clan. So we invited the Salvants to join us at 116 Peachtree Circle for a week, a month, whatever they needed.

The Salvant parents enrolled Duvey and Eugenie in the neighborhood schools and set about trying to find work. But one morning during the second week, after all four kids had left for school, Jennifer, the mother, pulled me aside. "Kevin, I just want you to know that our clothes are clean," she said, her Louisiana drawl trying to cover her embarrassment. "We wear the same three outfits all the time because we were packing like it was a camping trip. This is all we have."

I headed into my magazine office with Jennifer's words haunting me. Three outfits for weeks or months? Later that morning, at my business partner's urging, I fired off an e-mail to about thirty friends telling the Salvants' story and asking if they might contribute something to help this family. Two days later our mailbox at home began to bulge with envelopes, and soon I held thousands of dollars in checks.

When we gave the money to the Salvants, Jennifer's eyes filled with tears. So did mine when she hugged me.

Joseph and Duvey quickly became good friends, hustling home from school to throw balls around in their now-shared back yard. Many days when I was pitching baseballs to the boys, Eugenie would wander out, demanding, "Mr. Kevin, Mr. Kevin, look what I can do," her pronouncement followed by a cartwheel performed with the perfect enthusiasm of a four-year-old.

The Salvants ended up living with us for about three months. It was a sad day for us when they packed up Tim's van and headed back home to resume their own lives. But after they drove off, we began to recognize an opportunity to break our accumulating consumer momentum—and to see our house as something other than a residence. Maybe 116 Peachtree Circle wasn't just a piece of property. Maybe it had the potential to be used for the greater good. After all, it was one mighty big asset.

Beyond that, all four of us had been deeply involved in the experience of sharing our home with the Salvants. We had collectively cleaned rooms to prepare the basement apartment, hauled in furniture, and helped the family feel welcome. It was a team game, and we had played it that way.

As important, the sharing we had done really had nothing to do with writing checks. What Joan and I began to recognize is that as necessary as financial gifts may be, they didn't resonate with our kids. We parents might have been feeling good, but our kids weren't feeling much of anything.

There was a soullessness to the sort of giving we did, broken only at rare times, as in that three-month period when we invited the Salvants to share our space.

Jews call financial charity *tzedakah,* and it's a crucial tenet of the religion, as it is with many religions. But Jews have another charitable concept, *chesed* (pronounced *khehsed*), which describes good deeds done without cause, a proactive experience that isn't preceded by a request and usually involves more time than money. It often is considered to be a way to love with selflessness, a genuine generosity of spirit.

In reality, a kid's brain and heart can relate to acts of *chesed* a whole lot better than to the cash gifts of *tzedakah.* The trick for us was to satisfy all the elements. We needed to be doing something ourselves, instead of only writing checks for others to do things. We needed something the kids could feel. And it needed to be big enough for Hannah to believe that we as a family were "doing something," not just talking.

Looking at our life, we realized that we were a long way from living out the Dalai Lama's guidelines: "Think of other people. Serve other people sincerely. No cheating." How many of us can pass the test that those three simple sentences lay out?

Twelve months after the Salvants drove out of our driveway to return to New Orleans, we were gathered for our Chinese dinner in the breakfast room, sitting at the scratched oak table that Joan's grandmother had bought in rural Iowa decades earlier. My collection of contemporary art surrounded us like old friends; a portrait of an Asian woman crafted in steel pins sat behind my place. This time there was no e-mail to trigger action on our part, just Hannah's fresh memory of the homeless man and the Mercedes—and Joan's test. We waited to see the kids' reaction to her suggestion to sell the house, move to a smaller one, and give away a bunch of the money.

I think Joseph nearly fainted. After all, this was the only home he'd truly known, having moved here when he was five. The mantel of his bedroom fireplace was covered with baseball trophies and home-run balls (the one to left-center off Wesley, the two-run shot off Robbie). He had baseball sheets on his bed, and his bookshelves were lined with Harry Potter and Get Fuzzy books. This was Joseph's home field.

Far more than that, he questioned the rationale of something so dramatic. As he told me later, "I thought this was something theoretical, that it would never really happen. I mean, with the Habitat stuff we were doing and the other activities like the food bank, weren't we doing enough?"

As for me, I was slightly in shock. Selling the house wasn't a huge deal to me—Joan and I had always viewed it as just a nice piece of property. We don't get sentimental about houses as many people do. Joan's parents in Iowa have owned their home for forty years, even though as empty nesters for two decades they barely use several of the rooms. That's not how Joan and I view houses; they're nice to live in, we make them feel like us, but they have never defined who we are.

Still, the magnitude of Joan's challenge jarred me. Although we had in the past discussed moving to a smaller home, this was a different plan altogether. Attractive in some ways, but certainly a dramatic turn. We would be giving away hundreds of thousands of dollars, maybe as much as a million. We were talking about taking our most visible tangible asset and essentially cutting it in two—a chunk for us, a chunk for them. Whoever *them* was.

But Joan pushed on. "If you guys really want to make a difference, we don't need this large house," she announced, gesturing past the breakfast room to the ornate kitchen with its three Viking stoves and Portuguese inlaid tile. "Enough is as good as a feast. We could live in a place half this size, and use the excess money to really do something to help others."

There's an old joke about New York that goes something like this: "What's the shortest window of time in the world?" "The period from the traffic light turning green to a cabbie's horn honking." I think Hannah was quicker to jump on Joan's idea. "I'll give up my bedroom. Dude, we should *definitely* do this," she declared. "We should sell the house and give away the money. Definitely."

Recognizing Hannah's passion about the idea, Joseph started getting worried. Maybe this wasn't all so theoretical. "What? No way. Why?" he sputtered. He looked around the table, wondering, *Why is everyone getting moved so much by something we see every day, like the homeless guy?*

Joseph and I stayed quiet as Joan kept her focus on Hannah, making sure that she understood the consequences of what was being proposed. "Are you sure," Joan asked in measured tones, "that you want to move out of the house that has been yours since you were seven? And give the money away to help people we don't know? Are you aware this would mean giving up a bunch of your stuff—maybe half the things in your room?"

Hannah was, as they say in political circles, on message. "I want to do this," she repeated. "Let's sell the house and do some good with it. We don't need this place."

Across the table, Joseph helped himself to another bite of Mongolian beef, carefully avoiding the scallions. Joan eyed him, switching her gaze from Hannah, the big-hearted optimist, to Joseph, the now silent pragmatist. Feeling that he had slipped behind in this debate, Joseph figured it might be counterproductive to continue the conversation; this goofy plan would probably blow over. "I'm going to do my homework," he announced, picking up his plate and taking it to the sink. Maggie and our other dog, Charlie, padded behind him, hoping for scraps.

What Joseph and Joan shared without speaking was a recognition of magnitude. Selling a house is a pain; moving is a bigger pain. What we were talking about wasn't a one-time sacrifice but one that would take months of work, then a finality we'd have to live with and live in. Joan knew that this project wouldn't move forward without Joseph's buy-in, and she wasn't ready to force him into giving up his house without that. That battle would have to wait for another day.

With three of us remaining at the table, Hannah refused to take her foot off the accelerator. The opportunity to do something bold, to make a difference, was within her grasp.

She stared across the oak table, her eyes locked on Joan's. "We're doing this, right?" It was half question, half demand.

"I'm on board, Han," Joan replied. "But this will have to be a family decision." It was her way of acknowledging that, Joseph's reticence aside, I hadn't signed on yet either. They both turned toward me.

In the seven years since I left the comfort of the *Wall Street Journal,* my life has grown more adventurous. I started a company and became its largest investor, and when it succeeded, my partner and I decided to swing for the fences with a risky new magazine, all the while not taking salaries. I realized that uncertainty and transition, not knowing exactly where the path would lead, made me happy.

Sitting there at our kitchen table, under two sets of glaring eyes, I quickly processed the massive leap Hannah and Joan were suggesting. Frankly it sounded ridiculous . . . and fun. "Count me in," I announced, watching Hannah's face brighten.

As soon as the words left my mouth, I wondered if we had really decided something this outrageous so quickly. I still couldn't believe this turn of events. When we had moved into this house, we had done so in large part for the kids. They needed a place, we had believed, where the upstairs ceilings went to full height, where they could have friends sleep over, have the home that was a magnet for their buddies. But Hannah's eagerness to move showed that she didn't care about any of that. Even Joseph's silence showed that he was at least amenable. As Joan and I had barreled forward, accumulating, we had misread their emotions—and had never even bothered to ask. They didn't want the big Dream House at all. The inertia was shifting fast.

Whenever something major happens in our lives, I'm the one who tries to lighten the mood with a joke or a sassy pop-culture comparison. Sometimes it makes everyone laugh; sometimes they just roll their eyes. No matter. I can't help it. So as Joan and Hannah focused on the serious implications of busting apart our elegant lifestyle, my mind circled back to a scene in the TV show *Sanford and Son,* in which the father, Fred (played by Redd Foxx), points to the junk business around him and fumes at his son, "Who do you think I'm doing all this for?" The son, Lamont (played by Demond Wilson), replies, "Yourself." Fred shoots back, "Yeah, you learned something."

Sitting at the table, I knew how Fred felt. We had moved here in part for our children, but for our own egos as well. Joan and I wanted the Dream House. We needed the upgraded New Normal.

Later that night, as Joan and I were preparing for bed, she raised the question we were both thinking: "Hey, Kev, are we nuts?" In the back of our minds, we knew we could probably back out of this if need be. But I didn't say that at the time, and neither did she.

"Maybe," I mumbled through my toothpaste, "but it will be a heck of an adventure."

HANNAH'S TAKE

Realizing How Much You Have

IF YOU HAVE A FRONT DOOR, YOU HAVE SO MUCH MORE THAN people in the villages of Ghana. Imagine your family living in a one-room house made of mud, with no running water or electricity. Imagine never traveling more than a few miles from your home, always on foot. Yet the people in Ghana appreciate what they have, even though it seemed to me when we visited them like they had nothing at all. They take pride in their homes by sweeping them out daily, and they keep their clothes clean. People used to say to me, "You don't realize how lucky you are," and I would just brush it off. It was true, of course; I just needed to recognize it.

But realizing what you have can be tough. First you need to start by acknowledging that you have a good life. Reading books really helped me get started. I love reading inspirational books, such as *Your Ultimate Calling,* by Wayne W. Dyer, or *Timeless Wisdom,* by Gary Fenchuk. If you haven't seen the movie *Pay It Forward*, grab the DVD and some popcorn; it's very moving, and watching it with your family can spark good conversations. The YouTube video of Professor Randy Pausch's "Last Lecture" is great for those days when you need to keep your life in perspective. As the Roman philosopher Cicero once said, "Gratitude is not only the greatest of virtues, but the mother of all the rest."

And here's a great exercise to try: a gratitude letter. Dr. Martin Seligman, a professor at the University of Pennsylvania, offers this suggestion in his really smart book *Authentic Happiness*:

Select one important person from your past who has made a major positive difference in your life and to whom you have never fully expressed your thanks ... Write a testimonial just long enough to cover one laminated page ... [then] invite that person to your home, or travel to that person's home. It is important to do this face to face ... Bring a laminated version of your testimonial with you as a gift ... Read your testimonial aloud slowly, with expression, and with eye contact. Then let the other person react unhurriedly. Reminisce together about the concrete events that make this person so important to you.

This exercise will help you get beyond yourself, but I think you can take the process even further with an extra twist: think about what you could be doing in the next few years that would trigger someone to write that type of letter to *you*. Not that they will, of course; the important thing is trying to make an impact on someone as strong as the one made on you.

3

Deal or No Deal

— — — — — — — —

You can't cross a chasm in two small jumps.

— **David Lloyd George**

O VER THE NEXT TWO MONTHS, life interceded. Sure, we had decided to sell our home, but you wouldn't have known it by our actions. We fell back into scurry mode, accommodating Hannah's volleyball season and the early practices for Joseph's spring baseball team. My magazine business was struggling, so hunting for more investors was almost always at the top of my mind.

But on those evenings when things got quiet around the house or Joan and I headed out for a walk, I felt torn about the rationality of our hasty decision. On the one hand, there was a thrilling sense of anticipation and excitement: we were cranking up a remarkable project, a real adventure, a leap into the unknown. But there was also a raging sense of self-doubt that hung like fog. More than once I wondered, *What the hell are we thinking?* We had plenty of role models for those times when we had gone in the opposite direction, when we had opted for newer, bigger, cooler. And

TV ads continually preached how much better we'd feel if we owned the latest and greatest. But *nobody* we knew was doing something like this. What family with growing kids makes the choice to shrink unless there is job loss or some other trauma? Downsizers are retirees or empty nesters, not parents of kids in school.

And let's be honest, giving can sometimes turn into misgiving. Impetuous decisions to try to help someone on the street corner or at the front door can be so tempting . . . and oh so wasteful.

Two or three times a year, Joan and I talk about the night in June 1987 that we got engaged. But when we remember that evening, we rarely reminisce about how I proposed or how she accepted. Instead we recall how a man approached us outside our apartment on the Upper West Side in New York. He seemed friendly, so we listened as he explained that his car had broken down a few blocks away and his wife and young daughter were waiting with it. "Here's my ID card for the school where I work in Brooklyn," he offered. (He couldn't have known, but it was the next high school over from my alma mater, Midwood.) If he could have sixty dollars for car repair, he'd be so grateful and would send it back to us the next day. With little debate, I reached into my wallet and gave him three twenty-dollar bills; meanwhile, Joan wrote our name and address on the sheet of paper he offered up.

I probably don't need to tell you what came next. Each day we checked the mail for his payment. It didn't come. After three days we became dubious. After six days we knew we'd been swindled. So much for compassion, damn it.

45

But about two months later, a shocking thing happened. We were walking down Broadway near our apartment when a man stopped us; he seemed friendly, so . . . Wait a second, it was the same guy! He had the nerve to work the same neighborhood! To try to scam us for a second time! I was speechless; Joan wasn't. "You tried this same bullshit story on us a few weeks ago. I'm getting the cops," she blurted, frantically looking around for a phone or an officer. He ran off, and despite our anger we decided not to pursue.

When it comes to charitable giving, we all want to do right. But if we pause to consider our donations, two huge questions keep coming up: "How?" and "How much?"

Let's take "How much?" first. In other words, what's the right level of giving? Toward the low end of the scale, most people are familiar with United Way's once-a-year campaign, or "annual arm-twisting ceremony," as I teasingly referred to it during Joan's and my corporate days. That's when a company United Way captain drops by your desk, pledge card in hand, to ask if you'll agree to have a "fair share" of your salary deducted from your paycheck. United Way's guideline of fair share: one hour's pay per month, or roughly 0.5 percent of your compensation.

At the high end of the scale is the biblical tithe, literally "one tenth" in Hebrew. Some Jews and Christians still see this 10 percent rule as God's expectation for our responsibility to others. But for the vast majority of us, including Joan and me for most of our marriage, 10 percent is well beyond anything we'd commit to doing. In fact, the average American comes in a bit above fair share and well below tithe, donating roughly 2 percent of annual income—a rate, by the way, twice as high as in any other industrialized country.

I'm not saying that money is the only measure of generosity. Far from it. At Atlanta Habitat, we would wither without the more than fifteen thousand hours a year that volunteers give to build roofs or paint walls. And for me, the hours that I spend hammering nails into Habitat houses are certainly as meaningful as any check I write (although the organization may not feel that way, given my limited construction skills). As the philosopher Kahlil Gibran wrote, "You give but little when you give of your possessions. It is when you give of yourself that you truly give."

Indeed, the right volunteer opportunity, as I've mentioned, can be deeply meaningful, especially to children, with their limited appreciation for money but large understanding of "doing." Despite that, let's focus on financial charity for now, since money is easy to measure and offers a good snapshot of how some of the thinking has shifted recently.

Even with the stock market carnage of 2008, the wealth created over the past two decades has brought some radical new ideas to the world of charity. Of course, the eye-popping multibillion-dollar commitments of Bill and Melinda Gates and Warren Buffett have snared headlines, as have some of the good works by dot-com entrepreneurs. But some of the most creative philanthropic concepts have occurred below the radar. In some ways, what we're seeing is the flip side of *The Millionaire Next Door*; instead of the storyline focusing on assets, it is happening on the philanthropy front.

Take, for instance, the Boston-area group called Bolder Giving. The founders, Anne and Christopher Ellinger, urge people to donate *half* their assets to charity, regardless of income level. The Ellingers created the 50% League, comprising individuals who have donated half their income or business profits for at least three years or, alternatively, who give away half their net worth sometime during their lifetimes. Who's in the 50% League? A college professor, a Massachusetts candidate for governor, a relatively unknown TV and movie actor, a social worker. People you'd see on the street or in your local deli, all of whom have figured out what they actually need to live on and then given away the rest. The beneficiaries of their largesse: the environment, the homeless, education, and health care, among others.

At the same time, the California money manager Claude Rosenberg launched a nonprofit organization called the NewTithing Group. His conclusion: most of the strategies we use to determine our charitable donations are wrong. Rosenberg's team recognized that most of us eyeball how much to give instead of doing any math. Late in the year, we essentially take a guess at what we can afford to give away, then write a bunch of checks. Beyond that, people who actually do take the time to run the numbers mistakenly use annual income instead of total assets, including their investments. As a result, Rosenberg argued, people give dramatically less than they could, especially the wealthy. NewTithing set out to convince anyone who would listen that they should donate more of what they own, not just what they earn.

Despite the urgings of the Ellingers and Rosenberg, aggressive philanthropy is still a fringe sport. Rosenberg died in 2008, and his nonprofit organization subsequently closed; meanwhile, the 50% League has fewer than two hundred members. Perhaps there's a certain stigma on people who give too much during their lifetime. They're seen as eccentrics who don't know the value of money, or who are caught up in extravagant gestures rooted in some aversion to wealth. If people want to be extremely generous, the custom is to do it after death, leaving bequests to charity or a personal foundation.

What can we conclude from all this? For one thing, answering the "How much?" question is far more art than science. People who choose to give (and more than 80 percent of American households do) may end up *averaging* 2 percent of income but do so at a wild range of 0.5 percent or less to 50 percent or more.

If only "How much?" were the harder of the two questions. Unfortunately, "How?" is a killer.

Possibly the easiest way to illustrate that is to circle back to the homeless man Hannah and I saw at the Connector-Spring corner. What would solve his plight? Was he a drunk, or did he have mental health problems? Would alleviating his hunger with a few bucks soothe or hurt? What's the long-term answer for him to turn into a more productive member of our society?

It doesn't take many of those questions to make us freeze up or, conversely, just plunge unthinkingly into what feels right. After all, how are we supposed to give money intelligently to help that individual or the millions like him? Searching for the right answers (or maybe not even think-

HANNAH'S TAKE

What Can You Give Away?

NO MATTER HOW LITTLE YOU HAVE, IT'S WORTH PARTING WITH half of something in order to make a difference. You definitely don't need to be the Gates family to create a project of your own. Not even close. In fact, who says money is the only thing to give away? Sometimes giving up time is better than giving away money or clothes. If you cut in half the hours a week that you watch TV, surf the Web, or play online games and spend that time at a food bank or a soup kitchen, that time can really help improve someone's life.

Think about something that you do often in your free time. Chances are you would still be happy doing that thing a little bit less. In fact, I'm certain you'll feel happier. As the psychologist Dr. Maxwell Maltz once said, "Our self-image and our habits tend to go together. Change one and you will automatically change the other."

The point of this is not so much personal sacrifice as it is realizing how much you have available: time, talent, and treasure. In the evenings when our family worked together at the Atlanta Community Food Bank, not one of us was thinking of lost time on Facebook. I have never met a single person who has said that they gave too much or volunteered too often. Have you?

Activity

Sometimes people can't recognize their own strengths, and it takes other family members to help them realize they have extra that can be shared. Here's a way that we have used to determine the available resources of each member of our family.

Stack three different colors of index cards into piles, with each color representing time, talent, or treasure. Each person takes one card of each color for each other member of your family. (For example, if you have a four-person family, each person takes three green, three blue, and three pink, so a total of thirty-six cards are distributed.)

Each person writes time, treasure, and talent cards for each other family member. Then you read them aloud to one another.

As an example, here are the cards that I would make for my friend Aubrey if we were in the same family:

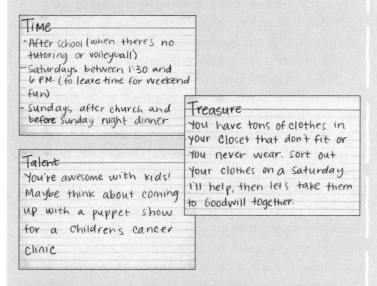

Time
- After school (when there's no tutoring or volleyball)
- Saturdays between 1:30 and 6 P.M. (to leave time for weekend fun)
- Sundays after church and before Sunday night dinner

Treasure
You have tons of clothes in your closet that don't fit or you never wear. Sort out your clothes on a Saturday. I'll help, then let's take them to Goodwill together.

Talent
You're awesome with kids! Maybe think about coming up with a puppet show for a children's cancer clinic

Once you've completed this activity, choose at least one from each of the cards you collected in the different categories. For instance, you might take the talent card that your sister made for you, the time card that your dad made, and the treasure card that your brother made. Then act on them.

ing about the questions), well-meaning folks do what they can to help. They drop a dollar into a cup. They volunteer at soup kitchens. They travel on mission trips, building wells or schools.

Not knowing what else to do, sometimes I even tried to make a game of it. Before I was married, my roommate Marc and I would go out to bars on the Upper West Side of Manhattan and, in the wee hours of the morning, stop on the way home at H&H Bagels to buy two dozen bagels. We would keep a dozen for ourselves and see if we could distribute the rest to panhandlers on the nine-block walk up Broadway to our one-bedroom apartment. I can tell you with certainty that we didn't change any lives.

For many years Joan and I thought often but shallowly about the effectiveness of aid. In a big city like New York, deep social issues were always right there, life-sized. Homeless people slept on grates outside our apartment. Friends contracted AIDS and other diseases. The mentally ill turned to the refuge of subway cars for shelter.

We knew that government agencies spent liberally as they tried to help these people and that faith-based groups and other nonprofit organizations worked to fill in the gaps. But people were still living outside our apartment. How could that be? The "How?" was so darn puzzling.

So when big-hearted Hannah announced at the dinner table that we needed to become a family that does more than just talk about doing things, all she knew was that something was wrong, that she wanted to help. At that moment she was a lot like the rest of us, eager to fix a problem, aware of disparity, but fuzzy about solutions. Surely if we gave of our time or our money, we could solve something, right?

Hannah had no idea that debates over how to repair humankind's worst ills have been raging for decades, centuries, millennia. One small example: Back in the 1980s, when Joan and I were living in New York, then-mayor Ed Koch announced that if compassionate New Yorkers really wanted to help homeless men and women, they needed to *stop* giving them money. Instead, he said, they should urge panhandlers to get help in a shelter equipped to take on the bigger issues. The mayor's edict was shocking to Joan and me. Stop giving? But that's how we helped. Now we were being told that it wasn't help at all but instead a hindrance.

Occasionally Joan and I would read an interesting article and once again debate the issues: Does our society have an obligation to educate the kids of illegal immigrants? Who has the right to health care, and who should pay for those who can't afford it? Are the auto companies failing society by producing gas guzzlers or simply responding to consumer demand?

Still, as far as our thinking connected to annual giving, we probably achieved no more than a five on a one-to-ten scale. Each December we'd flip over a piece of junk mail and make a list of the groups we wanted to support. Then we'd write checks to what we called "the Big Four": our alma mater (Northwestern), Joan's church, our kids' schools, and Atlanta Habitat. Totaling it all up, our answer to "How much?" was typically about 3 percent of our income, a bit above the U.S. average (though we didn't actually do any research to know that). Not huge, but respectable. And we had one corollary rule: if a friend sought help with a favorite cause, we'd write a check for fifty dollars, no questions asked.

Our giving was intentional, but only insofar as we knew we wanted to help our community and we felt we wouldn't miss the money. As our pay rose, the size of our gifts rose significantly (although as a percentage of our income, our giving declined). Still, we ramped up our contributions with a nagging hesitancy, harboring worries about regretting our generosity. Who knew what the future would bring? And we certainly weren't old-money patrons who could be counted on year after year for more and more.

But now, following our hasty dinner-table decisions, we had emotionally and unexpectedly made a monumental decision to dramatically alter our lifestyle. Without having heard Rosenberg's urgings to give based on assets instead of income, we had shifted gears.

There were so many questions. Could we live rationally in half the space and at half the price, creating for ourselves a shrunken New Normal? And if we couldn't, would the money netted from this project be significant enough to justify the work it would take to sell and move? Would this life change feel painfully sacrificial? How would a new space affect the personal dynamics of our foursome? We didn't have a lot of case studies. After all, who intentionally goes backward?

To begin to answer those questions, Joan quietly checked the Homefinder section of the *Atlanta Journal-Constitution* each Sunday for open houses in our neighborhood, visited, and inventoried what was for sale. For years Joan had attended open houses out of neighborly curiosity. But now she had a purpose: not to buy anything, but to learn if we were bungee-jumping with a poorly attached tether.

Frankly, it was easier than we thought. Even restricting her search to our current neighborhood, in just a few weeks Joan discovered that we could indeed get plenty of space for half of what our current home might fetch.

During this time we learned about some action on our old street, a hidden jewel called Walker Terrace that runs for only one block. The homeowners had taken their house off the market a few months earlier and now were getting ready to put it back on. Just our kind of opportunity: no agent meant no fee, and we knew the street well, so we understood pricing. We even knew the couple.

We certainly hadn't expected to buy a house before selling our current one. I'm willing to bet that smart financial folks everywhere are reading this and yelling, "No, don't do it," as if they're watching Harry Potter walk into the Forbidden Forest. But this opportunity was likely to vanish, we surmised, and there are only a dozen houses on the street. (Yes, financial people, I know, that's what they all say.) Irrationally, we decided to make an offer.

The negotiation turned out to be an amazing two-day sequence. First Joan went alone to see the sellers, with an offer in hand that would cut their former asking price by about 25 percent. There wasn't a lot of low-balling to it, more a recognition of what we could afford if we wanted to give away half.

One of the owners, Lori, is a beautiful dark-haired woman with an easy smile and a winning Texas drawl. She listened expectantly as Joan laid out our offer, starting with the sweeteners of our proposal: no contingency, quick closing date, cash deal. But when Lori heard the price we were proposing, it was clear she was balancing a desire not to hurt Joan's feelings with her immediate rejection. "Joan, I'm really sorry, but we've already turned down offers higher than that," she said.

Disappointed, Joan gathered her coat and turned to leave, telling Lori that she understood but that was about what we could pay. Lori looked truly puzzled and almost embarrassed to ask the question that was tugging at her. "Can I ask you something? Why are you selling your house anyway?" Lori asked. "It's the nicest house in the neighborhood."

Figuring she had nothing to lose, Joan laid out the story in all its schmaltzy detail: how Hannah wanted to use our house as a tool to help the world and how we wanted to create a legacy of giving as a family. "Hannah really cares about people, and there are a lot of people in need. We're going to research where to work, but it may be Africa, since there are so many needy people there," Joan told Lori. By the time she stopped speaking, Lori's demeanor had changed. "Oh my God," she said with a gasp. "Can you come back and tell my husband that story after dinner?"

Joan pulled out the heavy artillery for the return trip to see Lori's husband, Blair: she brought Hannah. In front of Blair, Hannah did what Hannah does. She delivered the passion. Blair opened by saying, "Lori has already told me that you guys are doing something interesting with the house. Hannah, tell me about it."

For five or six minutes Hannah told her story, barely pausing to breathe. It was pure emotion, heartfelt and raw, the kind of passion teenagers usually save for their dating breakups. Dressed in her Urban Edventure shirt, which she wore the first time she worked at Café 458, she spoke about her eagerness to combat hunger. "Ever since fifth grade, I've been really concerned about people who are served at places like Café 458. I've done a lot of volunteering there and at the Central Night Shelter and the food bank," she started. She then told the story of the homeless man and the Mercedes, and explained how she wanted to change lives. "If we sell our house and move into this one, we can use the profits to do more to help people."

As Hannah spoke, Blair stared in rapt attention. Hannah couldn't help but notice what Joan saw: our daughter was earning respect and admiration from a grownup.

When Hannah was done, there was a pause, and Joan asked Hannah to wait in the car while the adults talked. Out in Joan's Toyota, Hannah listened to hip-hop stations, while inside Blair and Joan discussed price and other details of a possible transaction. Our offer was too low, but the higher purpose for which we wanted the house gave us some additional currency. We hadn't known it until that day, but Blair confided to Joan that Lori had a dream of helping children in Africa and hoped that our project would lead there. The conversation ended with Blair asking if he could get back to us the next day; they needed to think it through overnight.

Joan and Hannah came back that night cautiously optimistic. The sellers seemed interested, they reported as we sat down for dinner in the breakfast room. We didn't recognize it at the time, but by that night's dinner, some two months after the Chinese meal that had launched our project, we were already falling into the roles that would define our family. Hannah was, of course, the spiritual muse and catalyst. Joan was the process manager, making sure we always had a logical next step. I was the financial coordinator. And Joseph was our skeptic. These were roles we fell into naturally.

We listened as Joan briefly recapped the conversation at Lori and Blair's house. It was too early to say for sure, but this deal just might happen. Listening carefully, Joseph had a two-tier plan. Dipping three-cheese tortellini into the marinara sauce on the other side of his plate, he started by playing defense. "Tell me why we're selling our house again," our skeptic half demanded, half asked.

For the past few years, Hannah and I have had a running joke about Joseph. Whenever he does something ill-advised or says something ridiculous, Hannah shakes her head, then turns to me with fake exasperation. "Y'know, Kevin," she says in his presence, using her best "parent" voice, "our son is such a mess."

She wasn't in that comical mood that night. Instead, she instantly became impatient. "C'mon, Joe, how many times do we have to talk about this?"

But I quickly interceded: "Wait, wait. I get where he's coming from. Hey, we don't even know what we're going to do with the money from the move yet."

Tensions calmed a bit, and Hannah and Joan more patiently offered Joseph a renewed argument for our move. Either he ran out of questions or he was just setting up for his second strike. "Okay," he said, "but I want a playroom with a foam pit in the new house." Aha. So Joseph had been calculating ways to parlay this downsizing for us into an upsizing for himself. As he wrote in his journal a few days later, "I would like to move to Blair and Lori's house because it would give me a large playing space, more organized sports equipment, and more places for things we enjoy doing, like playing Ping-Pong, a foam pit, and playing guitar, piano, trombone, and Guitar Hero."

Don't get me wrong—Joseph's move wasn't a total land grab. He knew that we were voluntarily parting with some serious money and half the biggest asset we had. But his mind went to the place where lots of kids' minds go: how can I make this more fun for myself?

After dinner the kids asked to be excused from the table and headed off to do their homework. "I guess we've got some work to do," Joan told me, referring to Joseph. I just laughed. Joseph was transitioning from boy to teenager. Part kid, part young man. He could care about the world and still want his foam pit, whatever the heck that was.

But Joan wasn't just commenting on Joseph's self-interested response to our charitable endeavor. As usual, she had a bigger idea in mind.

I stood up, brought over a bottle of Trader Joe's Charles Shaw Shiraz ("Two-Buck Chuck"), yanked out the cork, and filled two glasses. Joan and I have long disliked fancy wineglasses, because we hate to hand-wash dishes. And we've been blessed with palates that struggle to differentiate good cheap wines from excellent expensive ones. So, we drink bargain wines from juice glasses.

Joan took a sip of Shiraz, then started in. "You know how our kids haven't derived much from the community work we've done in the past? You know how they never feel like we do enough?" I winced, my mind circling back to that dinner after the incident at the Connector-Spring corner. That was awful, trying to justify ourselves to the kids.

But where was Joan going with this? "Yeah, so we're selling our house and moving," I replied. "What else do we need to do?"

"Well, the reason our kids don't feel like they're truly part of the process is because we make the decisions and then they participate," Joan pointed out, unthinkingly rolling and unrolling her red placemat. "We have to empower them, let them really own this thing."

"Okay, so . . . ," I said hesitantly. "Didn't we do that in deciding to sell this house?"

In her career at Accenture, Joan had specialized in helping banks achieve more benefit from the people who worked for them. Her clients, including Wachovia and Bank of America, relied on her to help orchestrate the people side of the business, from the way divisions interacted to how they were staffed. In short, she knew how to construct groups to make them more successful. And she had been thinking about our organization, our little team.

"Our kids need real authority, a real sense of ownership. They need to help guide this project with full voting rights. We might end up with decisions different from those you and I might make on our own, but I think we'll end up with something that we all actually believe in. Are you willing to go along with that?"

I recognized what Joan was proposing. In organizational design terms, we would be flattening the hierarchy, altering the balance of power in the traditional family structure. Forget the usual two parents in charge of two children—the order of authority in our household and every other family we could name. That configuration would be replaced by a horizontal line. One person, one vote; each counted equally.

I took a swallow of wine, processing Joan's proposal. This was uncharted territory. Joan and I both had grown up in households where the parents set the rules and the kids followed them. My parents might have had a miserable marriage, but I knew that when I misstepped—like the time when I rode my bike in the street when I was eight—my father would sit on the toilet seat cover, put me over his lap, and spank me, sometimes with a hairbrush. In Joan's house there was never discussion about whether to go to Sunday school or continue piano lessons. You did what you were told.

When Joan and I became parents, we raised our kids firmly, allowing for discussion but rarely debate. We rolled our eyes at parents who let their children run wild in stores or restaurants. We set standards for grades, created limits on TV time, banned video games from our house (although we finally caved on that last one).

Still, I saw Joan's logic here. Joseph and Hannah were giving up their bedrooms, their back yard, their prestigious home too. And we couldn't risk their losing interest or backtracking, leaving Joan and me to defend the decision to downsize. "It could make a big difference in how the kids perceive this project," she continued. "If they feel like this adventure is theirs, I think they would own it. Hannah already sort of does, but Joe might really step up."

We both were well aware of how hesitant Joseph had been about this project so far. Not only didn't he own it, but Hannah and Joan were pulling him each step of the way. When he went along, it was for family harmony, not from eagerness. And neither he nor Hannah had really been a driver of family activities related to charity. When Hannah acted, it was usually alone or with school friends; Joseph, by contrast, waited to be asked, then usually signed on.

I must admit I wasn't instantly drawn to this idea. I loved the concept that we could work on this project together, and I wanted the kids to feel empowered. But the stakes were so darn high. This was our home we were selling. This was our shot at doing something significant, and I didn't want to screw it up. And teenagers are so . . . well, teenaged. Their decision-making can be irrational, hormonal, impetuous.

Joan sensed my tentativeness, so she pressed on. "Okay, let me ask you this: what are your goals for this project?"

"Well, I want to make the world a little better. And I want a family legacy, something that reflects what we stand for," I answered. As the sentence left my lips, I knew where Joan was headed.

"And how can it be a family legacy unless the family makes the decisions? How can half the family be omitted from authority?" she asked. Then, to reassure me, she quickly added, "And you and I will have just as much say as they do, and we almost always see eye to eye."

I reflected on that for a few seconds, draining the wine from my five-ounce juice glass. Still, doubt kept gnawing at me. "What happens if the kids stop respecting our authority in other areas? You know what I mean? Can they feel like equals in this project and subordinate elsewhere? I'm definitely not ready to give up my parental responsibility in the family."

Even as I offered my protests, I sensed Joan was right. Power-sharing for this project was crucial. In fact, it would become the most important decision we would make, bar none. I just didn't recognize it at the time. In the end I offered a meek "Okay, let's try it and see how it goes," and little more.

It couldn't have been more than fifteen minutes later that our phone rang. Joan answered and quickly said, "Oh, hi, Blair." I moved closer to eavesdrop as Joan held the black cordless Sony near her ear. "Lori and I think we can make your offer work if you guys can come up a bit," Blair began, and I watched Joan's face brighten. Could we stop over the next day to discuss details and sign a contract?

"We're gonna have a deal!" Joan yelled up the stairs to the kids. Hannah hurtled down, taking the steps two at a time, demanding, "Tell me, tell me." Joseph finished another math homework problem before walking downstairs and into the kitchen. But as Joan told the kids about Blair's call, even Mr. Skeptical couldn't stifle a grin. This would be an intriguing new challenge, an opportunity for a fresh start. Even if he didn't feel it yet in his soul, Joseph could appreciate the opening of the curtain on the second act of our family's play.

But there was to be a twist to Lori and Blair's involvement. The next evening Joan and I traveled the four blocks to Walker Terrace while the kids were finishing their homework. Over that quarter mile, the neighborhood was the same, but the feel was like night and day. Peachtree Circle is a curving, arching boulevard, a main element of the vision that Frederick Law Olmsted, who also designed New York's Central Park, sketched into our neighborhood at the beginning of the twentieth century. Walker Terrace, by contrast, is a narrow, straight, cut-in street featuring a series of well-kept but nondescript homes. Even people in the neighborhood sometimes have trouble remembering it's there.

In our big house, guests walked up a curved drive onto a large wraparound porch. Often I would stand on that porch, football in hand, as Joseph ran elaborate zigzag patterns on the spacious lawn in front. At the end of his thirty-second pattern (a time in which an NFL quarterback would have been sacked, gotten back up, talked to his coach, and sipped some Gatorade), I'd throw the ball, trying to make him dive for that spectacular catch, maybe even a one-hander.

But as Joan and I walked up the twenty-foot brick pathway to the front of the new house, it was clear that there was no space for football here. The phrase "plain and simple" leapt to mind. A beige-painted brick structure, 18 Walker Terrace shares a driveway with the neighboring home. There were no gas lanterns, as at the bigger house, just ordinary bulbs to light the entryway. And inside there would be no kickoff dinners for fifty guests in business attire. There would be no boast to this house at all. Practicality would be the message.

Blair opened the front door. Nipper, the couple's Jack Russell terrier, sniffed us, then eagerly accepted a few scratches behind his triangular ears. After exchanging some pleasantries, Joan and I settled in the living room and hammered out the details of the contract with the owners. It took only a few minutes to agree on price, closing date, and the rest of the particulars. We signed, initialed, and dated.

Then Blair sprang the surprise. "We think what you guys are doing as a family is really amazing," he began. "It's definitely something that our girls are too young to understand. But sometime down the road we'd love to tell them we were a part of it."

Blair handed Joan a five-by-seven sheet of lined paper, handwritten in blue ballpoint. She squinted at the note, struggling to read the specifics of the scribbled print: "501(c) (3) . . . shall have the ability to direct." Two signatures at the bottom of the page. Through the chicken-scratch, one thing was clear: Blair and Lori had decided to contribute $100,000 to our project over several years. We had a deal, but beyond that we had something else: we had validation of our idea. Someone else had heard it—in fact, the only other people who had heard it—and not only thought it made sense, but had supported it with their own family assets.

Joan and I hustled home, the freshly signed contract and the handwritten sheet in our hands. We had barely pulled into the driveway when Hannah and Joseph appeared at the glass front door, eager to hear the news. Joan began to explain the $100,000 donation when Hannah spotted the handwritten paper. Even as she strained to read the writing, she exclaimed, "Dude, that's so cool, soooo cool." Joseph arched in closer to scan the page over her shoulder. "Yeah, that is cool, I gotta admit," he said, a smile coming to his face.

Hannah's eyes sparkled as if she had just snared a winner on one of those scratch-off lottery tickets that Santa gives our kids as a gag gift at Christmas. She reached across to high-five Joseph, who bounced a little, grinned, and accepted her smack.

Joan and I didn't have to take a vote from our newly impaneled jury of four. The looks on the kids' faces cast their ballots for them. We were unanimous about this one.

As the writer Charles Kingsley once said, "We act as though comfort and luxury were the chief requirements of life, when all we need to make us really happy is something to be enthusiastic about." At that moment, we knew what he meant.

HANNAH'S TAKE

Helping Small Kids Start Volunteering

I AM NOT A SMALL CHILD, NOR DO I HAVE ONE. BUT I DO know that the seeds of giving and caring in my life started to grow when I was young. When I was around seven years old, I started to see helping experiences as something of joy and as a way for my family to really connect.

For instance, on those Saturdays when my mom, my brother, and I took food to the Habitat for Humanity building sites to feed my dad and the other volunteers, the three of us would shop for ingredients, cook lasagna, and serve the workers. We couldn't build, but we had an important job. I began to realize that family experiences could go beyond obvious entertainment like an outing to Six Flags (although I still love going there).

One trick for younger kids, including me, is to find activities where there are quick, clear results. Dr. L. Richard Bradley, an Ohio specialist in service learning, notes that kids aged seven to ten "are most engaged when their efforts lead to immediate, tangible results, even on a small scale." I know that was true for me. For instance, my first real volunteer experience, at the Atlanta Community Food Bank when I was eight, was great for kids. Helping to sort groceries and learning how food pantries serve the hungry allowed me to really see the effect I was having on people in need. And it was a blast to check out the unusual kinds of foods that grocery stores donated, from cereals with movie themes to crazy shapes of mac and cheese. Because it was a good fit, I think it inspired me to volunteer more often.

A good site we've found for parents of younger children is www
.learningtogive.org (click on Youth Workers and go to the youth activities section). As the advice columnist Abigail Van Buren said, "If
you want children to keep their feet on the ground, put some responsibility on their shoulders."

Activity

Sometimes it's hard to find organizations that can use younger kids
as volunteers, but there are other ways that they can get started.

1. How about pulling your family together for a neighborhood park cleanup some Saturday? Make it a dress-up day
for you and the kids, with prizes for silly outfits or the person
who can have the least skin showing. Then grab those trash
bags and gloves and go.

2. Do a grocery store run and buy food for a soup kitchen
or food bank. Adults pick adult food; kids shop for their
peers. In my family, Joseph and I used our charity money
during these trips, so we also got to learn how much food
costs. Then we delivered it to the food bank together.

3. Most kids love pets, especially cats and dogs. Try ar-
ranging a family outing to visit the animals at the Humane
Society, adding in a contest for who comes up with the cut-
est name for a dog. Make sure before you go that the kids
know they won't be able to take a pet home, so that there
isn't a problem at the end. While having lunch or ice cream
afterward, talk about the fact that everyone and everything
needs love, not just people who have a caring family.

4

The Power of Half

— — - — - — - — -

Every man must decide whether he will walk in the
creative light of altruism or the darkness of destructive
selfishness. This is the judgment. Life's persistent and
most urgent question is "What are you doing for others?"

— Dr. Martin Luther King, Jr.

THERE'S A RUNNING BACK on Joseph's school
football team whose father likes to dangle the in-
centive of food. Really good, expensive food. During a recent season, each time Sam scored a touchdown his
father gave him a letter. Sam was trying to spell out B-O-
N-E-S, the name of the kid's favorite gourmet steakhouse—
average cost per head probably around seventy-five dollars.

In a game late in the season, an ugly loss against St. Pius,
Sam broke a second-half run around the left side and gal-
loped for the end zone. As our side's parents cheered this
small piece of good news in an otherwise lopsided game,
Sam's dad just sat on the metal bleachers with a grin on his
face. "Well, that's the S," he told me through his smile. "It's
time for steak."

That's not our family. When we want to celebrate, we eat breakfast for dinner. The night we signed the contract to buy the Walker Terrace house from Blair and Lori, Joan and I hustled home, fired a cursory question to the kids about their homework, then piled into the car and drove the 5.3 miles to the Atlanta Diner for our celebration dinner.

I'm sure you can picture the place: a shiny metallic outside, a neon sign shouting OPEN. We entered past the three-foot-tall ceramic waiter holding chalk-written daily specials and asked a waitress (no "servers" here) if we could sit in a section marked "Closed." We wanted privacy to start the work of our project.

We scooted into a horseshoe-shaped corner booth as the waitress dropped menus onto the clear plastic sheet that topped the green nylon tablecloth. As veterans of this dining establishment, we didn't need to open the menus. French toast (Hannah), French toast (Joseph), corned beef hash and eggs (Joan), open-faced turkey with gravy (me). Let's go.

Given the action of the past few days, Joan was eager to take the lead, to move into her role as process chief. She started by taking stock of where we were. The deal with Blair and Lori—not to mention their thrilling endorsement of the concept—had propelled our project to a new level. We weren't just talking anymore, we were doing. We were on the path Hannah had challenged us to walk.

Except that here in the diner, the kids couldn't stop talking, tweaking each other, clowning around. They were at their hyperactive best, talking about underwear and some kid at school and something on TV and where's the French toast and movies and Facebook. They were pure energy. As is often the case, I didn't do much to help, chiming in on their exuberant conversation and the physical activity that accompanied it. Straw wrappers were shooting across the table; the pepper shaker got knocked over. No doubt it was good we were seated in the "Closed" section.

Joan was businesslike. She asked a question. None of us paid attention. She grew impatient and asked again. Hannah made fun of Joseph's hair. In exasperation, Joan exploded: "You know, we're really not off to a good start here." Silence. Then more silence. Then a snort of laughter as Hannah tried to hold a serious face. Then all of us laughing, Joan joining in, realizing that we just needed to be having fun together at that moment. For about ten minutes our table was full of happy family chatter, no structure, no order; we were just enjoying each other's company.

When our food arrived, we settled down enough at least to speak one at a time. Joan, sensing the mood change, figured she'd try again to start us talking about how to use our forthcoming funds. "Let's say we've sold our house and we have a bunch of money. And let's say we decide to give away half of what we get. Would we want to help a few people a lot or a lot of people a little?" It was Question 1 in a sorting process that would take us a year to complete, our first baby step on the road to answering the "How?" in a way we could be comfortable with.

For the next hour Joan led us through a discussion of the biggest social issues on the planet. Hannah's passion may have started with homelessness on the streets of Atlanta, but a whole world of possibilities opened up from there. We touched on poverty (one billion people live on less than a dollar a day), lack of safe drinking water (at least the same number), homelessness (as many as 3.5 million Americans a year). On their face, the problems in the United States and the world were so daunting. As Joan recited data from articles she had read, Hannah, Joseph, and I took turns marveling at the size of the troubles. I'm guessing we must have said "No way" a dozen times during the meal, trying to wrap our minds around the magnitude of the issues.

I think that Joan's litany of world dilemmas might have sent other families running for the exit, certain that their potential to help was minimal. But we loved the quote by Anita Roddick, the founder of the Body Shop chain of environmentally and animal safe cosmetics: "If you think you're too small to have an impact, try going to bed with a mosquito." We knew, just *knew*, we could make a difference, even if it was a small difference. In fact, we think everyone can give of the three T's: time, talent, or treasure.

That said, our brainstorming conversation that first night reflected a whole lot of naiveté. At one point, as the waitress brought a small metal bowl with the extra powdered sugar that Joseph had requested, Joan began to talk about hunger. "Okay, listen to this," she said, glancing at an article she had torn from a magazine. "According to the United Nations, there are eight hundred fifty-four million undernourished people on the earth. That's about one in every eight. And a big number of them are kids."

Like every American child, Hannah and Joseph had tossed off the phrase "I'm starving" without thinking much about it; in reality, they were slightly hungry or just interested in eating. Their first introduction to more legitimate hunger had come during their volunteer work around Atlanta, when they met people who relied on social service agencies for free meals. Even that was confusing. "Those people actually look okay, don't they?" Joseph said. "I mean, you ever notice that some of them are even kind of fat?"

In response, Joan explained the nutritional shortfall of cheap, unhealthy foods. But beyond that, she noted, what we had all seen was far from the most severe malnourishment or unvarnished hunger. In the United States, hunger is rarely life-threatening, Joan pointed out; while the food choices of the poor are severely limited, and probably life-shortening because of their lack of nutrition, the food supply is ample. And our cities are filled with soup kitchens, food banks, and homeless shelters. "But in third world countries, there is no safety net, no way to get the kind of help that exists here," Joan continued. "The people we're talking about in India or a number of places in Africa are just desperate for anything to eat."

Without thinking, Hannah blurted, "Why don't we just put a whole lot of hamburgers on a plane and fly them over there?" I glanced at Joan, who was straining to stifle a chuckle. The table was silent as Hannah's question hung there. My interior monologue went like this: *Is she kidding? Hmm, she's not smiling, so maybe not. Hamburgers? Thousands of miles away?* After a few seconds, I decided to break the silence with a question: "And what would they eat the next day?" Another moment or two of silence. "Oh yeah, duh. What I meant was, I wish we could share what we have," Hannah said.

Like lots of families, we tease each other. If you can't laugh at yourself, we figured, who would want to spend time with you anyway?

Starting when Hannah was about five, I had told her a story that she had been left on our doorstep as a baby. "And pinned to your blue blanket was a note that said, 'Please take care of our little boy,'" I deadpanned. "Oh, Dad," Hannah usually responded, shaking her head and giggling. One day when she was about ten, after I'd repeated the yarn for the umpteenth time, her face became serious. "Dad, if you thought I believed that story was real, would you still tell it to me?" I refused to give in: "What do you mean *if* the story was real, Han?" I replied, straight-faced. "Oh, Dad." Then she belted me on the arm.

Hannah's hamburger blurt at the diner came, of course, from her enthusiasm, her intense desire to fix the wrongs she saw in life. But the rest of us wouldn't let that get in the way of a good razzing from time to time. "Hey, why don't we fly cheeseburgers over there?" Joseph would tease her at random moments. "First of all, it was hamburgers, not cheeseburgers, Joe. And by the way, you're an idiot," Hannah would reply, laughing and chasing him, sometimes to douse him with a plastic cup of water or punch him playfully.

We were under way, beginning to dig into our core values, individually and collectively. It was fascinating how involved we had been with charity in the past but how little we actually understood about making a dent in big issues. We could joke about Hannah's hamburger gaffe, but even Joan and I spent the next year being surprised time after time by the simple truths we didn't know. And that wasn't good enough; we needed to learn quickly. After all, the contract on the new house meant that we were past the point of no return. Our move was in motion, and nobody needed to take a vote to know we didn't want to squander an opportunity of this size.

At the diner, Joan began to probe, forcing us to dig into our deeper selves. She tossed out question after question: Do we want to work in Atlanta, elsewhere in the United States, or overseas? Are we interested in relief work or longer-term help? Should we look for social investments (like microfinance) that we can reinvest at the end? Or should we use the money on good works that won't have a payback but are badly needed? Should all our energy go to one charitable effort, or should we spread it around?

Joan didn't expect us to have many answers during that meal at the diner. She just wanted the questions on the table. And given the power-sharing pact with the kids that she and I had established, I made a point of refraining from my usual tendency to call out my answer and assert parental authority. Joan and I spent more time listening hard to the kids' answers and watching carefully when they spoke.

Joseph has a quirky method of cutting food, by holding the food with his knife and yanking a piece toward him with his fork. As a result, with French toast, he often tosses bits of powdered sugar onto his shirt. A father notices things like that when he's observing closely.

Several times Joan stopped for vote counts. At one point, as we were discussing poverty, I brought up India, explaining the desperation that Mother Teresa had found among the city dwellers in Calcutta and elsewhere. I barely got a second sentence delivered when I could see I had no shot in our newly formed democracy—one look at my fellow voters' faces made it clear that this proposal would never pass. "It seems much worse in Africa," Hannah said. "Those people have nothing, really nothing." "Looks pretty bad in Africa to me too, Dad," Joseph agreed. Joan was more blunt: "Yuck. I have no interest in going to India. I don't think we can handle those slums in Calcutta."

An hour into our meal, we ran out of steam. The kids began to squirm, and Hannah kept looking down at her phone to see who was texting her. Joan sensed this and quickly wrapped up the questions with a hasty "You guys done for the day?"

As we left the diner, we had reached two conclusions. First, we wanted to work on one cause in one place. Without Bill Gates–type money, pledging ourselves in multiple locations or with more than one objective would spread us too thin. Second, we had a lot of work to do. How and where to dedicate our resources remained huge unanswered questions.

Adding a major new commitment to lives full of the usual chaos wasn't something we relished. It's funny how nothing ever seems to come off the plate; more just keeps getting added. More lessons, more sports, more travel. And we weren't exactly the world's most organized people. A baseball friend once gave us a standing ovation for having Joseph at a practice ten minutes early, as the coach had mandated.

A few years earlier, late on a Saturday afternoon, I noticed that both our kids had sleepovers and Joan and I had no plans. "Hey, we're totally on our own tonight. What do you feel like doing? A movie or something?" So Joan and I went to a Thai restaurant, ate basil rolls and massaman chicken, and drank Singha beers.

The next afternoon our home phone rang. "Hey, are you guys okay?" our friend Susan wondered from the other end.

"Sure. How are you?" Joan asked.

"Married," Susan said.

"Oh, crap." We had totally forgotten our friends' small wedding; it had never crossed our minds. That was thoroughly, completely embarrassing.

Now with this new project, we were overlaying another huge to-do on four already overbooked people.

Fortunately, Joan had thought about that. "We're simply going to have to bring more discipline to our weekends. You know, find an hour to journal and talk. One hour a week," she said. "I think we can put down a marker for an hour that would easily just go up in smoke." For Hannah, that would mean a little less sleep. For Joseph, leaving the Xbox off. And for Joan and me, structuring a day that would protect that hour.

Joan's note in her journal reflected her concern that we could pull off the necessary time and emotional commitments. "Helping in a meaningful way takes a lot of time and patience. Like training for a triathlon or any other significant goal, parts of the work are less fun than others. Adult talk, long meetings." Could Hannah and Joseph handle the effort this project would take? Would we really all find the time?

The next day was a Saturday. Hannah had volleyball practice and Joseph was headed for baseball, so we huddled at nine-thirty for a half-hour chat about a topic we all dreaded: the tedious, often back-breaking work to prepare to move. We gathered in the living room, Hannah sleepily sitting next to me on the couch and Joan and Joseph propped in the lime-green contemporary chairs. Joan asked us to write for three minutes on "why I want to do this project." And there was a second question, she quickly added: "Write what you would be willing to sacrifice to make it happen—in other words, what work you'll do here in our house to make a difference in the world."

The kids pulled out their old-fashioned black-and-white composition books, the kind once standard in elementary schools. Hannah switched pens midway, from blue to black, after her first one ran out of ink, but her fervor poured out in both colors. "I think other people in the world need money more than this family does," she wrote. "I would give up a lot of things for this. I would give up five hours a week for working on getting the house together, and do homework during lunch (even though I'm very much against that). I would love to help fight for the 29,000 *kids* who die each day from starvation."

Across the room, Joseph turned his entry into a list titled "Sacrifices." He even wrote bullet points:

- Hard work
- Wake up earlier
- Help maintain cleanliness
- Help with eBay (to sell extra possessions)

- Smaller closet
- Smaller room
- No back yard
- Take dogs to park
- Throw away junk
- Yard sale

Then, at the bottom of the page, he added, "While I do not know what charity to give to, I like that we are sacrificing a bit of our own lives to enrich others."

In the next month we launched into the truly unpleasant work of move preparation. During our migration from Washington thirteen years earlier, I'd joked to Joan that I had come up with the world's best crime deterrent: don't throw the bad guys in jail; instead make them move every three months to houses of different sizes and furnish them. Pure torture. Beyond that, this move didn't hold the luxury of saying "Let's stick it in the attic and decide later." Downsizing offered no extra space. Half was half. All the rooms, all the items needed to be sorted into one of three piles: keep it; throw it out; give it to Goodwill.

That became our weekends, five-hour stretches of purging household goods to slim down to half size. We stopped talking about the amount we threw away or boxed up for Goodwill. Instead it became a game of pounds, as in "We lost a lot of weight today. Great job." Nothing about this felt much like service; it was more like garbage collection.

Still, group cleaning was essential, not just to shrink but also to keep our project a shared family experience and make the sacrifice real. We took turns reminding each other what we were doing and why. One day I came across a quote from the poet e. e. cummings that I read aloud to the family: "To be nobody but yourself—in a world which is doing its best, night and day, to make you like everybody else—means to fight the hardest battle which any human being can fight." Breaking out of standard accumulation mode had its moments of self-doubt; we needed the inspiration.

It surprised us how much detritus had built up while we were on autopilot. We'd never been collectors, carefully gathering objects of sentimental or financial value. Instead we had been accumulators, just bringing in more willy-nilly. Early in our married life, Joan and I had tried to live by the New York apartment rule: if something came into our home, something else of equal size had to be removed. In the days of our seven-hundred-square-foot Manhattan apartment, that had been a necessity down to the sock count. But as our lifestyle grew in the following decades, that maxim faded away, and our few edicts about what we or our kids absolutely couldn't keep—Happy Meal toys may not enter the house—did little to trim the clutter.

Now that we had decided to shrink, each of those hundreds or even thousands of items needed to be looked at, thought about, and decided on. Room after room after room. Boxes in the basement that hadn't been opened since the move nine years earlier. Do those headphones still work? Does that alarm clock just need new batteries? Does that shirt still fit? I'd hate to throw that out if it still works. Can it be recycled? Over and over and over again.

Each Monday night our rolling trash bin overflowed with garbage. Black lawn and garden bags of clothing and toys were stuffed into our cars alongside lamps and other large items for their journey to Goodwill. I remember one Saturday when Joseph had a baseball game in some far-flung suburb. On the way to the game, I erratically swung from the right-hand lane to the far left turn lane and quickly steered the Highlander into a strip mall parking lot. "What the heck?" Joan gasped. In response, I just pointed at the Goodwill drop-off door a few hundred yards away. "Good call," she said, glancing back at the pile of toss-offs we seemingly always had with us. The maneuver may have briefly put our lives in jeopardy, but we were purging more from the 6,500-square-foot home/storage bin.

That said, two positive surprises came out of the drudgery.

First, memories flooded back as we went through the kids' books, clothing, and old trophies from teams long forgotten. Joan and I learned what Hannah and Joseph treasured in their history, which T-shirts held meaning, what memorabilia mattered. We paused often to reread books our kids had enjoyed years earlier — *The Digging-Est Dog, Hazel's Amazing Mother,* and *Strega Nona.* Sometimes, when it was a little too quiet, we'd find Joseph sitting on his bedroom floor reading a Captain Underpants novel he'd long outgrown but still found worth a potty-joke giggle. We learned that our kids' teachers had "finished" (in other words done) a number of the art projects we thought were Hannah or Joseph's work. "Oh, Mrs. H did that one," Joseph said about a watercolor Joan and I had hung in our bedroom. We tossed it in the garbage, Joan wondering aloud what a kid learns from a teacher doing his art project.

In the middle of our purging, the least enjoyable part of the process so far, the second remarkable thing happened: Joseph became a full-blooded convert to the mission. Forget the entry he had written a few weeks earlier about "sacrificing a bit of our own lives to enrich others." As he told me later, "I kind of wrote what I thought everyone else wanted to hear." Even though he hadn't read it aloud, he felt that political correctness was the right strategy for that journal entry.

But here in Purge Week #3, Joseph actually stepped outside himself for a moment and began to look at his life through fresh eyes. It was the tedium of losing house weight that did it. "On something like the second or third trip to Goodwill, I realized that I was a pack rat. I had all of this stuff that I didn't use, things from when I was two years old," he recalled as we were driving months later. "Besides, we had a whole floor of our house we didn't use and a back yard we hardly used anymore. Who needed all that? It was way more than 'enough.'"

While he retained his outward skepticism and didn't tell us about his change of heart until more than a year later, the rest of us began to feel a softening in his ambivalence. Joseph wasn't being pulled into our efforts as much, and often led the purge with an energy that no one else shared.

One weekend we held a yard sale. Our goods were strewn about the lawn, while Hannah and her friend Aubrey tried to draw traffic by dressing in absurdly mismatched outfits and waving signs saying YARD SALE—HALF PRICE. The girls were giddy and exuberant, but our merchandise was iffy. We tried to sell nine baseball bats, none of which was the right size and weight for Joseph anymore. One of them sold. We had less luck with our old TVs and stereo speakers, all of which I later drove to Atlanta's electronics recycling facility, twenty-five minutes away, wondering on the way back whether they were just going to be thrown in the dump anyway. Candy Land and some hundred-piece kids' jigsaw puzzles remained, along with crutches from Joan's knee surgery, placemats too formal for the new house, candlesticks, DVDs, king-size linens.

When the sale ended, the excess had to be hauled off or given away. Now I was the whiny one. Loading all the leftovers into the car, I found myself blurting out what I figured everyone felt. "This whole moving thing totally sucks," I fumed. Joseph was carrying a stack of old board games toward the Highlander's hatch, staying in motion as he seemed always to be during these hours of purging.

As I glanced at him, my brain flashed to Joseph over the past three weeks, working long hours, pushing to get closets finished so we wouldn't have to revisit them. He might have logged more time than any of us. Now, despite this longest of long days, the guy was upbeat. "Hey, we made almost five hundred dollars today," he chirped, dropping the load into the Highlander and heading back for more. This move might not have been Joseph's idea, but he embraced the challenge.

In part bolstered by Joseph's newfound energy, we felt confident enough to break the news of our family project to some of our closest friends. It didn't exactly go as we had planned. Far from it.

Joseph had been born less than a month after we moved to Atlanta in 1994. We had few friends and no family. But one late summer afternoon, Joan took two-year-old Hannah and newborn Joseph to our neighborhood park. There, a dark-haired mother with a daughter four days older than Hannah approached to look in the stroller at Joseph. "You have a gorgeous baby," Della Wells cooed to Joan.

Our families' fifteen-year friendship blossomed from there. Every weekend we gathered for Sunday night dinner at one or the other's house, sometimes bringing dogs along to share in the fun. We attended the other family's sports events and life milestones; we shared Easter dinner, Passover seder, and Mother's Day; and we created traditions, including goofy plays and dance routines by Hannah and her new best friend, Aubrey. We became the Salwells, friends in name and family in spirit.

A few weeks after we signed the contract to buy the Walker Terrace house, we headed out to Park City to ski with the Wellses. During one of our purge days, Hannah had raised the idea of telling the Wellses, even though we were still early in the process and hadn't yet nailed down all the details. "How can we not tell them?" she asked. So we collectively decided to break our exciting news during the ski trip.

The second night in a rented condo, our octet of Salwells sat down at the pine table for a dinner of spaghetti and salad. We had traveled as a group of eight for nearly a decade and had settled into a comfortable routine. Della loved to cook, so she packed a huge black suitcase stuffed with pasta, cereal, granola bars, premeasured spices, even whole chickens. We nicknamed that piece of luggage "the chuckwagon," sometimes more formally dubbing it Charles Wagon for our amusement.

As usual, our accommodations were decent but not extravagant. In Park City, this condo felt much like the rest of them, with plenty of neutral colors, a fake stone fireplace with old wooden skis crossed on top of it, and a photo of the moon rising over a generic ski mountain.

I sat at the head of the table, Joan to my right. We had decided to tell the Wellses our big news, but there had been no rehearsal, no clearance of presentation. I guess we figured we'd just offer up our reasoning and the Wellses would be excited. What wasn't to love?

As soon as the blessing was finished, Joan spoke.

"We have some news," she began, her voice trembling just a bit in a mix of excitement and nerves. She looked around the table at her family and close friends. The condo-supplied dishware held steaming portions of pasta. The chrome salad bowl was still making its way around the table. The girls were piling on oversized portions of Parmesan cheese.

"We're selling our house and moving."

She didn't get another sentence out. From across the table, Della's expression dropped. "What? What? You're leaving us?"

We quickly deteriorated into a chaotic muddle. "Well, no, no," Joan quickly replied, "just over to Walker Terrace, our old street. You remember it."

Hannah talked over her. "We're moving into a smaller place so we can help people with needs, maybe in Africa."

I tried in vain to clarify. "You see, Hannah and Joan have cooked up this scheme to sell the house and move and it's only four blocks away."

"Our idea is to give away half the money," Hannah announced.

All the articulate clarity Hannah had mustered for Blair a few weeks earlier was gone. Together we stumbled for a little while longer, then stopped.

There was silence from the other end of the table, as all four Wellses tried to piece together the story. Della's face relaxed as she realized we weren't leaving town, but there had been little logic in our makeshift presentation; after all, we didn't even know where the money was going, although Africa came up in seemingly haphazard ways several times.

Finally Jere, Della's husband, swallowed a bite of garlic bread, smoothed his mustache, as he often does when he's thinking, and spoke. "I get that you're selling your house and moving. But tell me again *why* you are doing this?" Jere was my cigar-smoking hot-tub buddy on these trips, the guy who probably knew me as well as anyone in our adopted city of Atlanta. But our pronouncement had come from nowhere, and he was genuinely baffled. "I mean, what's the point?"

Again Hannah, Joan, and I started a cluster reply about our project and the plan to work with impoverished people. Joseph alone didn't try. He just sat, lightly dipping his spaghetti into the marinara sauce on one side of his plate, shoveling forkfuls of pasta as the rest of us struggled to come up with the magic words in the right sequence.

At last Joan was able to package our collective thoughts

rationally. "Okay, it's like this," she started, taking a sip of water. Then she went through our thinking sequentially, more or less coherently explaining how we wanted to do the seemingly simple: swap a big house for a smaller place and invest half the resulting money in people who could live better as a result. She pointed out that we had more than we needed and could easily part with some of our many possessions if it made others' lives a little better.

Now there was a foundation to have a logical discussion. In the end, the Wellses were more than pleasant about it—Jere asked me to talk to a class he was teaching, and Judson, their seventeen-year-old son, offered to help us move. But we came off sounding flaky and impetuous. Without thinking it through, we had delivered jarring news poorly, muffing our announcement to our closest friends.

Our communication got worse before it got better. When we returned to Atlanta, we told Joan's parents and my mother in New York. Joan's mom, June, is deeply anchored in her own history, and I mean that in a good way. Her friends have been her friends for decades; her home in Iowa has been the King residence since 1968. "You're selling the house Hannah and Joseph grew up in?" she said, startled by our decision. My mother focused more on where we were considering doing our work: "Africa? Why Africa? Do you know how much need there is in Appalachia, right here in the United States?"

A couple of days later, Joan had breakfast with another longtime friend. Over eggs and hash browns, she explained our plan, this time working hard to organize her thoughts better. When she had finished, she paused to let her pal react, waiting for the "How cool" or "Wow, great idea." Instead, when Joan looked across the table, she saw nothing but her friend's moist eyes. After a few seconds, the woman finally spoke, softly, haltingly. "This is not my family's reality. We could never do anything like this," she said. And although she offered to involve her family in our project, it was clear that the discussion, at least for a time, had put an uncomfortable distance between the two women.

This was blowback none of us had expected. Our project was creating a moat—at least a temporary one—between us and people we cared about.

Half an hour later, Joan pulled the Toyota into the driveway and marched through the front door, not stopping to pet the eager dogs. "That's it!" she yelled to the house at large. "We are not telling anybody about this anymore. No one, you hear? I'm sick and tired of feeling like a weirdo."

Our new communications strategy became "just shut up." We turned inward, focusing on our family's work. It had become clear that the audacity of this project was offputting to people, who took it as a challenge to their own lives or values. It made them feel uncomfortable and in turn made them perceive us as an oddity. "I had expected that telling my friends about this would bring us closer," Joan told me later. "Instead I was embarrassed—it was so awkward." Our overhaul of the New Normal clearly didn't feel normal to anyone else. Who needed that? Just shut up.

We couldn't cloak the fact that we were selling the house, of course; we just stopped telling people why. Instead, we explained that we no longer needed the extra space for live-in child care or the parties Joan and I had hosted in our corporate days. A true story, just not the real story. Some people might have thought we were having financial difficulties, but we figured that was better than dealing with the "Are these people from Mars?" looks we had seen.

Before we put our house on the market on April 1, we hired an independent appraiser and asked several real estate agents for advice on price. Then we listed it, "For sale by owner," for $1.95 million, a number at the consensus. Joseph walked the streets of the neighborhood dropping fliers about our open house into mailboxes and under doors. More than thirty people came to see the property that first Sunday, including the *Trading Spaces* star Vern Yip (no deal; he wanted more view of the Atlanta skyline). Despite lots of interest, no real offers came that weekend, or during the following month. In May we listed the property with a real estate agent.

Even though the house hadn't sold, our family's energy level stayed high. Joan and I took on the roles of information-gatherers, trying to make our biweekly discussions around the glass dining room table productive. One major piece of the big puzzle—where we might use our money—turned Joan into a research machine. Her file folder bulged with torn-out magazine articles, dog-eared copies of books about big social issues, articles printed from Web searches. She gathered dozens of data points for our meetings.

During that time I stumbled across an academic field that didn't exist two decades ago: youth philanthropy. There have long been organizations aimed at helping young people build character by doing good; the 4-H Club, Camp Fire Girls, and Boy Scouts were all created in the first two decades of the twentieth century. (Hannah joined the Girl Scouts but quit after several years when she tired of cookie sales.) For decades those organizations offered a way for civic-minded families to instill good habits into each new generation.

Then, in the 1990s, the deaths of fourteen students at Columbine High School in Colorado helped fuel concern that even children growing up in what seemed like "good" families could go horribly off-course. I talked about this with Luana Nissan, the director of the Glenn Institute for Philanthropy at the Westminster Schools (which Joseph attends). After Columbine and other rampages, she explained, it became clear that some of America's young people "led a life disconnected from a number of socializing influences."

In response, anxious parents demanded that schools adopt the kind of character-education programs long considered to be the purview of religious private schools. One by one, thousands of American school systems started adding to their curriculums such programs as Character Counts, which features "six pillars of character": trustworthiness, respect, responsibility, fairness, caring, and citizenship.

Hannah and Joseph had received a fairly strong dose of character and service education at Westminster and Atlanta Girls' School. Early on, Joan and I read through handouts about the "character trait of the month" and tried to put their recommendations into action at home. But life often got in the way, so the activity handouts often ended up beneath a pile of mail or other papers. It wasn't until Hannah was old enough to seize the initiative that our work became more energized.

On the home-sale front, all around us we could feel the housing market beginning to weaken. But we didn't worry. After all, we told ourselves, we were selling a unique property, one perfect for a family like we used to be, growing and accumulating. We just needed a buyer like us a few years earlier, someone eager for a 6,500-square-foot house, someone ready to live larger.

Week after week, with each call from Sally George, our real estate agent, about a prospective buyer, we herded up the kids and dogs, tidied up the house, and headed out. The process reached a new level of absurdity in the late spring, when Joan had knee surgery forced by a fall during that ski trip with the Wellses. Two days after she had returned home from the ligament reconstruction, I helped carry her to the car, her bandages oozing blood and ointment. She sat in the passenger seat for nearly an hour while the prospective buyers walked and talked their way through our home. Those lookers didn't buy either.

We came close once or twice that first year, with two offers that came in more than $200,000 below our asking price. When we countered the proposals, the bidders walked away. As summer turned to fall, the economy continued to weaken. Companies stopped hiring. The stock market got skittish. Homes stopped selling.

Back at my media company, investor dollars dried up. I hadn't taken a salary for two years, as several of us plowed cash back into the magazine and website, hoping for a miracle. In many ways, magazines are about dreams and fantasy; you'll never have a living room like that in *Metropolitan Home* or a body like that in *Shape*, but you can dream. My business partners and I had a dream too, to build a company that would help businesspeople foster careers that had as much focus on purpose and passion as on profit.

As the largest investors in the company, Joan and I were eager to make that entrepreneurial dream come true. But by fall 2007 it was clear that Motto Media wasn't going to make it. The decision my partners and I made was harsh but inevitable: since we had more than $600,000 in debt and no real options to raise more capital, we closed the business. Seven years of money, sweat, and love—gone.

You might rationally wonder at this moment, *What on earth are those people doing? A failed business, an unsold house, a part-time teacher's salary, and a plan to hand over half the value of their home?* Fortunately, our stock portfolio was holding up all right. And even more fortunately, our family philosophy of refusing to dwell on what we couldn't fix held up even better. Through all the stresses of business and home, we began to look forward to our family meetings, eager to push the project along.

At one Sunday get-together, Joan handed out an eight-page packet printed on the back side of paper she had brought home from school. As the kids and I settled into our white dining room chairs with the gold-woven cushions, she stepped into Process Lady mode. "Here's what you need to do," she announced, sounding very much like the seventh-grade teacher she was during the week. "I want you to look at the list of issues on the first page, then circle the four that are most important to you. Then let's call them out and I'll put them on the whiteboard."

Her list was divided into two sets of problems, broadly split into "Poor People's Issues" and "Everybody's Issues." In the first category she listed such ills as hunger, homelessness, lack of clothing, inability to read or write, lack of job skills. There were eight in all. "Everybody's Issues" also featured eight items, ranging from drunk driving to smoking to cancer to racism to the environment. We got to work on that top page, circling, thinking, circling some more.

As Joan dutifully tallied the results on the whiteboard propped against the mahogany buffet, only one of the concerns drew unanimous circling, "lack of water to drink and wash with." We spent the next fifteen minutes filling out the rest of the packet, reacting on a five-choice scale of "strongly agree" to "strongly disagree" to such statements as "It is important to target the money to people who live nearby, since there are many people in need here in Atlanta" and "It is important for us to visit and see how the money will be used rather than simply give it to an organization we trust."

Then we talked. For over an hour we debated the relative merits of helping the neediest cases versus those that needed a boost from the second rung (say, emergency nutrition packets versus a new library). The question of whether to help the worst-off with the funds from this project triggered strong disagreement.

Joan, Joseph, and I each gave the idea medium to low marks. "I'm thinking about some of the mentally ill homeless men Dad and I have seen for thirty years on the streets of New York and Washington and Atlanta," Joan told the rest of us. "I worry whether working with them might be too disheartening and probably something we could never finish."

That concept irritated Hannah, coming from her idealistic perch. She had offered up a five, the most positive grade. "The neediest people are the people who need our help the most. They have the least chance of succeeding," she pointed out. "Maybe we can't help as many, but we know we could help them."

"What would happen if we helped just one or two people with all our money?" Joseph wondered aloud. "That might be cool."

"Dude, I don't want to do that," Hannah replied. "That seems like a waste, to spend it all on so few people. But I don't want to give up on truly needy people either."

And so it went, all of us revealing a bit more of ourselves as the afternoon went on. We sat, we stood, we argued, we learned, we lay on the rug, we brought each other water and Diet Cokes. We listened and shared our sometimes differing, sometimes parallel visions.

Early in the afternoon's discussion, Joseph noticed that Joan had mistyped the word *unsure* on the worksheet, accidentally adding an *s* to make it *sunsure*; then, through the efficiency of cut-and-paste, it appeared as *sunsure* on each sheet. As the dialogue went along, he teased Joan. "Hmm, I don't know, Mom. I'm just so *sunsure* how I feel about that," he said, trying to hold back laughter. We all used *sunsure* for days after that.

There were no computers, no phone calls. Scheduled activities were off in the distance. In earlier times I might have checked my e-mail to make sure sports fields were open. Hannah would have texted friends, ironing out plans for the week. Joseph would have been reading the Sunday comics.

But we relaxed and trusted Joan's process. The questions concerned our passions and goals, not specific projects. We simply couldn't have made a rational decision about anything that specific at that point. We just talked and listened, learning where we agreed and where we didn't.

Probably unconsciously, many of Hannah's ideas about our project that day mirrored her thoughts about what our family should be. For instance, in response to the worksheet statement "It is important to target the money to solve a problem completely rather than to be part of something bigger than our dollars can solve," Hannah circled the five (for "agree strongly"). Then, in big printed letters at the center of the page, she added this sentence: "When you start something, finish it." We would face the completion test a number of times in the coming months and years.

All in all, I found myself marveling at our kids' capacity to debate issues. They cared about the world—yes, even Joseph, the skeptic. They thought more deeply than we had given them credit for. To heck with the house and the business—I liked where our family was headed. I wouldn't give this up for anything.

HANNAH'S TAKE

Starting a Family Conversation

MANY PEOPLE TELL ME THEY CAN'T BELIEVE HOW MUCH MY family talks about issues. This can be especially shocking for people who often know my silly side. But for my family, dinnertime brings us together during crazy weeks filled with school and sports and work. Even if your family is rarely together during the week because of conflicting schedules, make sure to have meals or time together over the weekend. Then the trick is to find something that every member can have an interest in.

In our family, we look for ways to expand events into discussions. For example, a TV show about a celebrity's mansion I saw one night led to a conversation about why Americans (including us sometimes) become fascinated with celebrities. A couple of things I saw online gave me plenty to think about and discuss with my family.

If the environment is your thing, try going to www.thestoryof stuff.com and watch Annie Leonard's video about where the products we consume come from and what that does to the earth.

Regardless of your passion, just try to get the conversation started with someone in your family.

When my family began discussing the deeper issues of the world, my parents started listening when Joe and I spoke. They were open to new ideas, and in these conversations they tried hard to make us all equals. They made an effort not to be bossy and they listened with open minds.

For instance, one night at dinner I brought up a school assembly speaker who had described the genocide in Darfur. My parents didn't try to educate me immediately on what was going on there; instead, my mom quickly grabbed a story about Darfur that she had seen in the newspaper that morning and read a bit to all of us. Joe threw in what he knew about Darfur, and suddenly we were talking — really talking. I think we stayed at the table at least fifteen minutes longer than usual that night because we felt connected.

Activity

Sometimes it's really hard to know what will spark a good conversation. Nathan Dungan of Share Save Spend (www.sharesavespend.com), a website that teaches kids about money, has some great ideas in his packet of "Discussion Starter Fun Cards." Some are better for younger kids, some for older. For example:

- How would you feel if you spent half as much on gifts (birthday, holiday, etc.) this year?
- If you were to give more money to a charity of your choice, what cause or organization would you pick? Why?
- How does immediate gratification get in the way of giving away money?
- If you can only give what seems like a little bit of money, why give?
- When have you bought something that you didn't really use or enjoy once you had it?
- If you inherited $50,000, what would you do with it?
- What is the best thing about sharing?

5

If You Don't Know Where You're Going, Any Road Will Take You There

—————————

If someone listens, or stretches out a hand or whispers a word of encouragement, or attempts to understand a lonely person, extraordinary things begin to happen.

—**Loretta Firzaris**

I F YOU'RE LIKE ME, you grew up watching TV commercials highlighting the miseries of hunger in Africa. The images were indelible: children with flies swirling around their faces, bloated bellies, ribs clearly pressed against chests. Near the end there was usually a small child with puppy-dog eyes, as the voiceover delivered the ask: "For just twenty dollars a month, you could provide relief to this child. Won't you just pick up the phone and help now? A desperate child is waiting."

I remember watching those ads on Sunday mornings during breaks in Abbott and Costello movies on Channel 11 in New York and feeling the pull to help those kids, an urge similar to the one Hannah felt on that day at the Connec-

tor-Spring intersection. What I didn't see was the stagger-
ing amounts of money being spent to try to solve the problems.

I was born in 1958. In my lifetime the Western world has
shelled out over $2.3 trillion to aid less-developed coun-
tries—with about one third of the funds going to Africa,
health, and education. Two point three trillion dollars. A
two, a three, and eleven zeroes. That works out to about a
hundred years of Kenya's total gross domestic product. Or,
taking Hannah's concept of flying hamburgers over there,
the West could have fed Africa's nearly 1 billion people a
McDonald's double cheeseburger each day for more than
six and a half years (assuming the sandwich was on the dollar menu).

It would be laughable if human lives and serious money
weren't at stake. Listen to this: despite the breathtaking flow
of funds for clean water, health care, and food, a United
Nations study shows that the average poor person in sub-
Saharan Africa now lives on seventy-three cents a day—less
than in 1973. All that aid, and people are actually *worse off*.
The conclusion is unassailable: we have poured most, if not
all, of that $2.3 trillion down the (nonflushable) toilet.

Clearly the big plans have failed miserably, as William
Easterly, a New York University professor, notes in his won-
derful but bleak look at the West's efforts with international
aid *The White Man's Burden: Why the West's Efforts to Aid the
Rest Have Done So Much Ill and So Little Good*. Easterly ar-
gues persuasively that the "Planners"—the World Bank,
the International Monetary Fund, and the economists who
have misguidedly spent so much of the money—attempted

to bring big centralized change to places that couldn't handle it. These were often countries whose long histories of colonialism—and associated exploitation—had given way to indigenous rule by an assortment of tyrants. In countries that lacked any responsible control over their own future, the arrival of tremendous amounts of foreign cash resulted in corruption and mismanagement; even worse, food and medicine never reached those who needed the help.

That wasn't all. The West, in its paternalistic, know-it-all way, consistently believed that it had not only superior technology but also a better sense than Africans of precisely what Africans required, from malaria nets to fertilizers to roads (roads, by the way, that fell into disrepair because the "lucky" recipients didn't request them or know how to maintain them). And life didn't improve. Anne Hope and Sally Timmel, writers and grass-roots community builders, refer to the third world as the two-thirds world, because two thirds of the world now belongs to it.

All of those well-intentioned but ill-conceived series of flops made our family nervous. This was our shot at making a difference, and the track record in the places we wanted to work in was discouraging, to say the least. I'm not a particularly good sleeper anyway, but I found myself popping awake at 2 A.M. thinking about hundreds of thousands of our dollars disappearing without creating any lasting value. It often took more than an hour for me to calm down enough for sleep to return.

But we didn't want to quit. Instead we set out to find success stories.

It had now been a year since our initial conversations at the oak breakfast room table. During that time we had gathered for roughly fifteen meetings over DiGiorno four-cheese pizza or bagels and cream cheese to kick around issues or vote on one of Joan's worksheets. The process Joan had put us through was something of a hybrid: we learned as we went, then voted on what we'd learned. And we often used car time together not just to listen to Top 40 radio but to chat about how our lives were changing or how to fix big problems.

I started to recognize our kids' curiosity growing about complex "adult" issues. During one Saturday morning errand run, I mentioned that I was headed off to preside over an Atlanta Habitat dedication later that day. Hannah and Joseph had attended these events, which are held on the last building day as a way to celebrate the completion of the house, thank the volunteers, and welcome the homeowners to inhabit the new residence.

This time the kids were more probing. "How much does it cost to build a house, Dad?" Hannah wondered, reaching forward to turn the radio down a bit to hear my answer.

"About seventy-five thousand dollars," I said.

"Where does that money come from?" she followed up. And for ten minutes we talked about Habitat's financial structure: how companies or faith-based groups cover the costs and how the homeowners pay zero-interest mortgages ("What interest do we pay?" Joseph asked). In that short car ride, we touched on charity, home finance, and our mortgage. Not bad.

Over the course of the year, Joan's process had led us to make some increasingly concrete decisions:

- We wanted to work in Africa.
- We wanted to take a project from start to finish.
- We wanted to join up with an organization that was already doing great work, instead of starting our own.
- We didn't want to join the Planners—in other words, to connect with some big United Nations program or some such. Instead we wanted to back Searchers, entrepreneurs experimenting with grass-roots strategies that empower local people.

Within our family, we remained three and a half strong: Hannah and Joan never wavered from their desire to push forward, and I was eager to see where this project took us. Joseph knew from his room-clearing Goodwill trips that he could do well with less and that the world needed what he had beyond "enough." He believed in the mission. Still, despite his advances in the first few weeks of purging, his daily life revolved around the affluence of his school friends, a group so fully ingrained in consumerism that morning time around the locker commons was frequently spent debating the best cameras for shooting movies or thousand-dollar paintball guns.

Joseph lived with a foot in each camp. At home he played a valuable role in our discussions of, say, the relative merits of giving malaria nets to African mothers or charging them a nominal fee so they would value the nets more. At school, meanwhile, he was right in the middle of conversations about the latest iTouch technology. Often he would bring the consumerism home, with birthday and Christmas lists full of gaming systems or other multihundred-dollar gadgets.

Joan and I pondered how to engage him even more fully —or whether we should. If he wasn't ready, he wasn't ready, I said. But one day, thumbing through *Instructor* magazine, Joan stumbled across something that might give him a renewed sense of drive: Coldwell Banker and Scholastic (the publisher of *Instructor*) announced a competition for elementary- and middle-school students titled "My Home: The American Dream." Each entrant needed to create a media project (artwork, comic strip, movie, and so on) explaining why his or her home was the embodiment of that dream.

This was a match made in heaven. Joseph loved making movies and already had posted more than a dozen mini ones on YouTube, from skateboarding adventures to "Nathan's Amazing Shot," a minute-long montage of a Ping-Pong ball ricocheting off a series of obstacles until it made its way back onto the table. Now he could make one that focused on our home and our family's decision.

The two-thousand-dollar prize Coldwell Banker dangled enticed him all the more. He had only one problem: as he sat down to sketch out the script, he realized that our family's American Dream was far from the kind that a real estate company would embrace. What kind of self-respecting real estate firm would celebrate downsizing? The big bucks went in the other direction. Joseph wasn't deterred by this realization; he intended to win.

Suddenly it was Joseph asking the questions at our dinner table. With his script in mind, he prodded Hannah on her motivations, asking more about that morning with the homeless man and the Mercedes. One Saturday morning in November, I found him sitting at the granite kitchen counter, blue dry-erase pen in hand, writing out cue cards on sheets of lined primary-school paper. He asked if I'd hold the camera as he told the story.

On that windy late autumn day we headed out to the front yard of the Peachtree Circle house, me holding Joseph's cue cards in my left hand and the JVC camera in my right. Joseph read from the cards: "Hi, I'm Joseph Salwen, a thirteen-year-old seventh grader at the Westminster Schools in Atlanta, Georgia, and this is my house [pointing a thumb behind him]. But not for long. You see, we're selling our house in order to finance our version of the American Dream . . ." Cars drove by, messing up the sound. The wind blew, so the cue cards folded over. Joseph stumbled over the script. We even shot multiple scenes with the camera on the wrong setting, which put us back to square one.

Joseph and I drove around town, filming the Atlanta Diner, the Buford Highway Connector, and even an apparently homeless man resting on a low stone wall, his belongings splayed out before him.

Late that afternoon, Joseph sat Hannah in a lime-green living room chair at the Peachtree Circle house, his camera settled on a tripod for stability. With light streaming through the windows and halogen bulbs overhead, Mr. Movie Director's lighting was good. Hannah was dressed in a white spaghetti-strap tank top with a strand of pearls she had borrowed from Joan; her auburn hair was neatly brushed.

"How did this project get started?" Joseph asked, pushing the Record button as he began.

It was a question she would be asked hundreds of times during the next year or two. But this early, she was as shaky as when we had told the Wellses the story in Park City. She breezed through an explanation of the homeless man and the Mercedes but struggled again to describe how we had decided to work in Africa and what we hoped to achieve. She rambled about "what I could do to help and how I needed to help . . . and we want to make sure people have a better life for good and never be hungry again . . . and how maybe other people will join us." It was one enormous run-on sentence.

Joseph stopped the camera. "Hannah, we need short sentences, otherwise I can't edit it. Think first, will you?"

He shot five more takes after that, but in try after try, Hannah's passions were clear but her thoughts weren't. "What should I say, Dad? This is horrible," she asked plaintively at one point. Clarity hadn't yet caught up with eagerness. Finally, on round seven, Joseph got what he needed and Hannah gratefully got up from the chair. "Why was that so hard?" she asked in exasperation.

That night Joseph edited the movie, connecting scenes, adding some slow-mo, and, naturally, incorporating humor and a little teasing of his sister. About one third of the way through the film, he dropped in a still photo of Hannah fully decked out in volleyball shorts and kneepads. His voiceover was hilariously terse: "This is Hannah. Hannah's my sister. One day she got outraged about hunger and now we're selling our house."

After three days of shooting, splicing, and refining, Joseph proudly showed the rest of us his work; he seemed certain he would win the contest. But his confidence was tempered by a critical stumbling block: "I have no idea how to end this thing," he told us.

We were gathered in the master bedroom. Joan had been doing laundry, and stacks of T-shirts lay folded atop the jungle-print comforter. Joan hates to match and fold socks, so a pile of them were plopped in the middle of the bed, waiting for someone else to sign up for the chore.

Joseph's quandary seemed easy enough to answer. After all, didn't he just need to reiterate why we were doing this? But his sentence triggered a forty-five-minute discussion about why we had undertaken this project and what we hoped to achieve. It should have been a no-brainer. But it wasn't. On the contrary, it took us back to some of the original exploration of how we started down this path—in other words, to our foursome's desire to stand for something, to build a family legend, to amend Paulo Coelho's concept in The Alchemist.

As I sat there in that bedroom listening, I realized that we were experiencing a critical facet of the process. We needed to remind ourselves of what we were doing and why. Reiteration not only helped us to reprise our mission and goals, but it allowed us to move forward from a common point.

Beyond that, we knew we needed to get the message right. After all, this was our first time talking about this in public in seven months, after the series of explanation misfires in the spring. We didn't want to sound cocky or arrogant or preachy. We were eager not to be perceived as strange. And we had become acutely aware that sloppy communication of our project could make others feel less charitable in their own efforts. How could we make sure others saw us as like themselves, to be encouraging without being uncomfortably challenging? After all, handing over half a house wasn't something most people were prepared to do, and we didn't expect them to.

As we spoke, Joseph took notes, stopping the conversation from time to time to tinker with his movie. He added clips and voiceovers. He experimented with background music tracks ("Bluegrass, anyone?" he asked with a laugh, knowing how silly it sounded). He showed us outtakes of himself stumbling over his tongue.

Soon it was midnight. Hannah was sprawled on the couch, nearing the end of her ability to participate. Polo shirts lay draped over the sofa arm, cramping her, but she didn't care much. "Joe," she said, "you just have to remind people why we started it and what it means to us. Oh, and then add something good at the very end so that, hopefully, people will do their own project or maybe join up with us. I'm going to bed. Good night."

The next day Joseph and I headed over to the Walker Terrace house with new cue cards in hand. First I walked across the street to ask a workman cutting tile if he was nearly finished, so the whine of his saw wouldn't overwhelm Joseph's closing lines on camera. Then Joseph sat on the steps, and we shot take after take of the script he had written that morning. In take number six, he nailed it: "So we're show-ing that you can redefine the American Dream to mean that sharing can lead to a better life for others. That's the Ameri-can Dream for our family. What's yours?"

He burned the finished film to a DVD and mailed it off with the entry form.

Three weeks later we headed for New York. Through our re-search and with help from Chip Raymond, the former head of the Citigroup Foundation and now a private adviser to donors, we had winnowed the hundreds of nonprofit orga-nizations working in Africa to four we thought were right in line with our shared vision. We had moved from "We want to help" to "Here's how we want to help." Therefore, just be-fore Christmas we traveled to the Big Apple to meet with three very different organizations. (We would do a Skype interview with the fourth one later.)

Hannah and Joseph had just finished finals, so for a few days they squeezed in a few sleepovers, slept late, and watched intelligence-sucking TV shows. As eager as we all were to move forward with our project, they needed a little downtime from the pressure of school.

But we were excited that we'd shrunk the pool of poten-tial partners to four, and each of us took one group to sum-marize for the others. We read brochures and other litera-ture, watched promotional DVDs, and wrote notes on the back of the manila envelopes the material had come in. ("Where do they get the doctors to put in the hospitals?" Hannah wondered on the back of one of the envelopes.) Then we presented our findings to the others.

As we waited at the AirTran gate for our late afternoon flight to New York, we squeezed together to watch videos several of the groups had enclosed. Freedom from Hunger, a Davis, California–based group, had engaged Jane Pauley as its spokeswoman. Joan and I, of course, knew her from her *Today* show days, but the kids didn't—and didn't care. "That woman is so annoying," Hannah exclaimed less than sixty seconds into the film. But as Pauley explained the group's strategy of empowering women entrepreneurs through microloans, Hannah softened. And when the anchor concluded that "a world without hunger is possible," our group was impressed. "Pretty good," Joseph said, pushing the Eject button on the MacBook and loading in the next video.

The reaction to Action Against Hunger, which had tapped Mandy Patinkin to host its pitch, was harsher. At first we laughed as we recalled the actor's role as a Spaniard in *The Princess Bride*. ("Hello, my name is Inigo Montoya. You killed my father. Prepare to die.") Joseph, a moviequote machine, tossed out more lines from the film: "You seem a decent fellow. I hate to kill you."

Finally we started the video again, listening more carefully to Patinkin's argument for Action Against Hunger's work. The group's focus was quite different from that of Freedom from Hunger, focusing on the toughest, most malnourished people on the planet, in war-torn countries, famine-stricken areas, and communities in crisis.

But our mood quickly turned sour as the video showed an African boy sitting bleary-eyed while flies swirled around his face. As an Action Against Hunger doctor described the child's lack of saliva and tearless crying due to malnourishment, Hannah couldn't bear the disturbing image. "What's wrong with these people? Can't they wipe that fly away from the poor kid's face? Oh my God, please, just wave the fly away, then go back to filming. Please!" she fumed. "I can't watch any more of this." And she left to get a drink of water from the fountain two gates down the C Concourse.

A few minutes later the AirTran gate agent began to call rows, and we put away the laptop.

The next morning began in standard New York fashion, with bagels and cream cheese, then we hustled across to Chip Raymond's Union Square office, settled into his light-gray conference room, and readied for our meetings. For the next three hours we met with nonprofit groups that all believed they had the right answers to the problems of Africa. What was remarkable was how different their philosophies and methods were.

We sat with yellow legal pads in front of us on the square walnut table, with bottles of Deer Park water available to quench our thirst. And the kids had their questions ready; in particular, Hannah wanted to ask about why each organization thought its strategy would yield better results than the trillions of dollars already wasted in Africa.

Millennium Promise brought an impressive team of four. The executive director, Jeff Flug, sported a long history at Goldman Sachs. John McArthur, No. 2, was a rising star in the anti-poverty scene. Joan and I recognized much of our younger selves in the team—we described them as "people like us," or at least like people we wanted to be. They were good-looking, they were charismatic, and, most important, they were guided by the vision of Jeffrey Sachs, the

A-list star of the aid world. Sachs had helped the UN craft the Millennium Development Goals (eight metrics to reduce extreme poverty by 2015) and had been named one of *Time* magazine's 100 Most Influential People in the World in 2004 and 2005.

Sachs's concept for saving Africa and other impoverished regions was a form of the shock therapy he had helped deliver to post-Communist eastern Europe. Poverty in Africa, he believed, could be alleviated with malaria nets, higher crop yields, microloan services, clean water, and improved health care. For these improvements to work, though, they all had to be delivered at once, not piecemeal. One big blast of aid.

On its face, Millennium Promise had it all: a can-do spirit that mirrored ours, $50 million in fresh pledges from the billionaire investor George Soros, and great pedigrees in both the business and the nonprofit worlds. But from our perspective, its strategy missed in one significant way: it relied too much on giving Africans the solution. While the concept of drenching poor communities with a wave of multidimensional aid sounded good in theory, we questioned whether the top-down strategy was all that different from the $2.3 trillion that had preceded it. Was it just a new-fangled version of "We're from the West, we're here to give you the answer," which had propelled failed international aid for decades? In short, the answer to Hannah's question "What's different?" wasn't satisfying.

Next up was Action Against Hunger, the group from the Mandy Patinkin movie we had seen in the airport. Talk about starting in a hole. We had shut off the promotional film, grossed out by the flies and the reality that famine or war-triggered crisis can bring. But Action Against Hunger won us over with props and amazing dedication. First, one of the organization's team, James Phelan, lugged in a gas can full of water that he had carried from the group's offices. "Go ahead, pick it up," he challenged us. "That way you can see what African women and children need to do several times a day as they carry water from the river to wash or cook with." Joseph, full of underutilized energy anyway, instantly popped out of his chair and hoisted the thirty-pound can all of about six inches off the ground. "Okay, that's seriously heavy," he said, laughing. We each took a turn.

Phelan and his boss, Nan Dale, spoke for about fifteen minutes about the kind of relief that Action Against Hunger delivers, focusing on the organization's work in nations with civil unrest or natural disasters. Many of the group's volunteers had been killed or injured trying to take aid to war-torn communities and desperately trying to serve the malnourished. It was sobering; this was the painful work of aid workers in the toughest spots on earth.

Then came the second prop: a bar of Plumpy'nut, a food that Action Against Hunger uses for children whose bodies are so emaciated that they can't absorb nutrients in any other way.

"Go ahead, try it," Phelan said, smiling as he pushed the bar across the table.

"No way," Hannah the starchitarian announced.

"Uh, you go ahead, Dad," Joseph said, wary of taking a bite.

"Oh, c'mon, guys, it's food—they feed it to people," I said, more boldly than I felt. I took a dime-sized nibble. "Pretty good, kind of chocolaty and peanut buttery," I announced. The kids reached out, eager now to snare some. Joseph decided that Plumpy'nut tasted "kind of like a mushy Snickers."

Water cans, Plumpy'nut, and then the most effective tool of all: before-and-after photos. As Phelan placed the photos side by side, we saw the powerful impact that aid can have, nursing starving children back to a semblance of normalcy. Maybe it was the props, maybe the mission, but as we compared notes between meetings, we realized we all loved Action Against Hunger.

Then there was our appointment with Joan Holmes, the founding executive director of the Hunger Project. No props. No pizzazz. No superstar. Not even any notes. Her style was passionate yet soft-spoken. We really had to pay attention to get the entire message. But what a message it was.

To understand Holmes, it helps to know that at the same time I was watching those hunger commercials in New York in the early 1970s, she was seeing them across the country in San Francisco. But her reaction was far different from mine. She didn't sit in front of the TV and try to decide whether to write a check; instead, Holmes wondered why the world's food-distribution system had become so broken and whether there were ways to fix it.

That was Holmes's way. A trained school psychologist, she was only six months into her first job in education when she became disillusioned with how her Seattle school system handled troubled students. "The default position was always that the child was the problem," she told me later. "But that's mostly because the child was the weakest person in the system." Searching for alternatives, Holmes built programs for gifted children and children with learning issues, and even served on a board to desegregate Seattle's schools.

Her skills and background brought her to the attention of three men intrigued by world hunger issues: the singer John Denver, Oberlin College president Robert Fuller, and the founder of est, Werner Erhard. The three had met through est, which Erhard launched in San Francisco in 1971 as a very early entry in what we now know as the personal development movement. And the theory behind est, jarring at the time but so remarkably mainstream now, is that people can be the authors of their own destiny, that we can empower ourselves to take any path we choose.

Denver, Fuller, and Erhard believed that conquering world hunger required many of the same skills that est training preached; success was a matter of encouraging people to fulfill their own destinies. In 1977 they tapped Holmes to create and run the Hunger Project.

Her first efforts to understand the roots of world hunger shocked her. She thought back to those commercials, with their pitiful collection of children. How many people died from hunger? she wondered. So she called the United Nations to find out. No one knew. There were no data, nothing that classified hunger as a cause of death. Amazingly, diarrhea was on the list, but not hunger.

As Holmes probed, she became even more aghast at the way the developed world approached poverty in the less developed world. First, there was no belief that hunger could be ended; it was seen as a problem that could be relieved in some places, but not ended. When the Hunger Project announced that it believed world hunger could be defeated, even other aid organizations objected, Holmes recalls.

Her second realization was far worse: that aid was not only misdirected but actually turned into *part of the problem*. The aid community had never distinguished between famine and chronic persistent hunger. As Holmes and others at the Hunger Project looked at the situation, "we realized that ten percent of the problem at that time was famine, a shortage of food for a short period of time. Famine is devastating, and that's what we were all seeing pictures of, people who really were victims." But the other 90 percent weren't famine victims at all, but lived in environments of chronic persistent hunger. "These are the women, men, and children who go out to work sixteen hours a day every day but are still malnourished," Holmes realized. "It's not that they are sitting around waiting for food. They are working their hearts out, but the opportunity they have is so diminished, they really cannot succeed."

From an aid perspective, that's a whole lot more than splitting hairs. If you treat people in situations of chronic persistent hunger as if they are suffering from short-term famine—in other words, if you keep bringing them supplies—they never learn to take control of their own future. Instead they grow accustomed to being treated as recipients or even victims.

In all of our research over the past year, no one in our family had ever thought through the differences between those two categories. Even though we had hosted victims of Hurricane Katrina in our basement, we had never considered what would happen if we had offered the same relief to them in better times. Viewed through that lens, of course, failing to differentiate between relief and long-term solutions seems ludicrous.

What the Hunger Project recognized was that people needed to be the authors of their own future. Africans needed to solve the problems for themselves, with support from Westerners in indirect ways. And women needed to be the leaders of that change. This was a philosophy we could believe in.

Through all three hours of meetings with the various organizations, Joan and I were fascinated. The kids, by contrast, were virtually comatose. It's easy to forget that kids don't do meetings; adults are so accustomed to these events that they are our standard of face-to-face communication. By the time our three hour-long sessions were over, Joseph had raided Chip's office kitchen twice and had eaten half a family-size bag of pretzels, not because he was hungry but because he was bored. His yellow pad was full of doodles of blocky men in fighting positions or skateboarding. Hannah, meanwhile, took notes just to be doing something, but her thousand-yard stare betrayed her fatigue. She peeled the label from her Deer Park water bottle strip by strip, meticulously folding it as she went. By the time the meetings concluded, Hannah and Joseph had nothing left. Joan and I agreed there would be no votes that day or the day after, as we returned to Atlanta.

Christmas came and went, and we rolled into the new semester of school. There were brief conversations about our New York meetings and several follow-up calls for due diligence, but we made no decisions.

Several weeks later, on a Thursday afternoon, after the kids had returned from school, we settled into the living room sofa for a Skype conversation with the last group, Freedom from Hunger, the California-based organization that had created the Jane Pauley video. When I say "settled into," I mean it. This conversation started with a brief description by the Freedom from Hunger team of their vision and programs. Then Hannah asked how their methodology differed from the $2.3 trillion of waste.

But as the video chat went on, the kids sank deeper and deeper into the couch cushions. At one point I elbowed Hannah (off-camera, I hoped) to keep her engaged. Joseph was snacking again to stay awake. (We have since joked, "What is it about discussing hunger that makes Joseph so hungry?") Finally, after about twenty minutes, the kids crafted some excuse about homework and asked to leave the meeting. Joan and I finished several minutes later, but it was clear that the format had doomed Freedom from Hunger's chances.

It was time to decide. The following weekend Joan brought the whiteboard and a set of colored dry-erase markers downstairs. Along the top of the board she listed the names of the four organizations, and then she wrote a series of questions that would help us decide:

- Who is in control, the West or Africans?
- Can we have enough impact with our amount of money?
- Can we complete a project?

Then she spread the printed materials for each organization across the blue scalloped rug for easy reference.

We agreed quickly that Millennium Promise gave too much control to Westerners, so it was the first organization eliminated from contention. Not a lot of debate there. From that point, the discussion accelerated.

"I'll go first," I announced. "I love Freedom from Hunger's HealthKeepers microloan program that helps African women build businesses and create healthier villages. It's like a twofer." But the kids expressed concern over the idea, noting that we could fund only a portion of the initiative. Check marks and X's began to fill the whiteboard.

Hannah argued in favor of Action Against Hunger's emergency relief program. ("Maybe we should just buy a zillion bars of Plumpy'nut," she said, fully aware that it would harken back to her hamburger comment.) Joan countered that the year-long worksheet process had positioned us to take a program from start to finish in a self-contained community. Moreover, in our year of talks and study, we had come to agree that serving those at the very bottom of the opportunity ladder wasn't the most rational place for us to invest;

instead, we believed that individuals a half step up, living in a stable country, had the best chance to use our capital to build a bright future. More check marks and X's.

Joseph contended that he didn't really care. "I hate to sound like I wasn't paying attention or something, but I think all these groups are doing good things and I think we would be happy with any of them. I really mean that. How about you, Mom?" Joan paused for a moment to figure out how to score Joseph's statement.

"Well, I want to talk about the Hunger Project," she said. "The mission is right, the method puts Africans squarely in charge, the focus on women's empowerment is the right answer, and I love the people running it."

The kids often tease Joan for listing, but there was little to debate on this list. Hannah looked down at the Hunger Project packet on the floor. Months earlier she had written a note on the back of the manila envelope: "The more I read about this organization, the more I like it." And she had added a smiley face.

We quickly batted around the question of how we could adopt two sets of villages, roughly twenty thousand people, in the Hunger Project's five-year program that moves communities from poverty to self-reliance. It would be a long-term commitment that would last until our kids were out of high school, I realized. As a foursome, we could connect with the same people year after year. But, critically, the villagers would be in charge of their own futures—not us, nor anyone from the West, for that matter.

"I kind of like that idea," Hannah said finally. "We could

really get to know people in the villages over the five years and see how they're doing."

"Should we vote?" Joan asked. She took a count, but by that point in the discussion it was obvious that we were unanimous. We would partner with the Hunger Project.

HANNAH'S TAKE

Tapping into Anger

SOME OF US KNOW RIGHT OFF THE BAT WHAT WE WANT TO get involved in. Whether it's orphaned children, global warming, or abortion, some of us just know our thing. But for those who haven't latched on to something yet, one great tool to determine the answer is to think about what makes you really angry. We care about issues because our gut says, "This is unfair—I should fix it."

There are two ways of getting to that answer, bottom up and top down.

First, bottom up: in other words, seeing someone and realizing that the topic goes beyond that individual. Jen, a friend of mine at Atlanta Girls' School, has cerebral palsy. She cannot walk or use the bathroom on her own, and most people at first cannot understand her when she speaks. When I asked her about her life, she told me that she gets weird looks daily and has to deal with people not knowing how to act around her. Yet Jen has the highest grade point average in my grade. She is also absolutely hilarious and can make anyone laugh. Because I am friends with Jen and know how much she has to offer, I get angry over the injustices she faces. If I hadn't already been so involved in hunger and poverty issues, I could see myself working on behalf of finding a cure for cerebral palsy, fighting for the rights of the disabled, or working with the city to make sidewalks more handicapped accessible.

Now, top down: in other words, looking at the big picture first. When we started our project, we were blown away that there were a billion people who live on less than a dollar a day. It was outrageous

121

how deep the poverty problem was, and, frankly, it was wrong. But we knew we couldn't help a billion people, only a few of those who were in that large group. So we looked for answers to help some in ways that might be copied by others.

Activity

Ask family members to list three topics that they are potentially interested in. They should try to tap into their anger about an issue or imagine how it might feel to be in another person's shoes. They can work from either the bottom up (if they have an individual they care about) or the top down (if they care about general issues).

Within three weeks, ask them to research each of their topics and prepare a one-minute speech in which they pretend to be the global spokesperson for that issue, trying to convince others that this is the world's biggest problem. They will need to come up with facts, photographs, and figures that demonstrate what will happen if this issue is not addressed. Have fun with it! Dress for the part, and maybe have props. This will make this activity more enjoyable and motivating.

6

Outside the Comfort Zone

Are you placing enough interesting, freakish, long shot, weirdo bets?

—Tom Peters

I N THE MIDDLE of our weeks of interviewing and sorting nonprofit partners, we moved out of the Peachtree Circle house and onto Walker Terrace. Unfortunately, most of our furniture never relocated. Many of the items were the wrong scale for the reduced quarters, while other pieces literally didn't fit. We didn't move any of our living room furniture or the round glass dining table where we had held so many family meetings. Buffets and armoires and couches stayed behind, as did the bed in the master bedroom that had been our group reading spot. Every room, and just about every piece of furniture, held memories, but we took the memories and very little of the stuff with us as we closed the door at 116 Peachtree Circle.

That said, we didn't sell the excess furniture, either. We had to stage the . . . Okay, I'll say it: the still unsold house.

(Time to cue the smart financial people, who have my full permission to crank up the "I told you so's" again.)

Our home had now been on the market for nine months. Potential-buyer traffic had slowed to a crawl in the deteriorating economy. Open houses were sparsely attended. We lowered the price by $100,000, but there was no denying the reality: we were the unproud owners of a "cold house," the kind that just sits with no buzz, no excitement.

You might say we were now experiencing the power of double—or maybe the curse of double. Two houses, mortgages, insurance policies, sets of utility bills. Talk about a self-inflicted wound.

I don't want to leave the impression that we were hurting badly. All around us, friends lost jobs, foreclosure signs popped up, people helplessly watched their retirement accounts slip to a fraction of their former value. We continued to volunteer at the Atlanta Community Food Bank and heard frequent pleas about replenishing soup kitchens' thinly stocked pantries. And in my role on the Atlanta Habitat board, I saw many of our homeowners struggling to keep up with their financial obligations.

Our family never stopped recognizing how fortunate we were (and are) to be healthy and to have flourished early in our careers. We weren't dot-com billionaires, but we certainly had more assets to live on than others.

That said, owning two houses was becoming a costly embarrassment. For years, as Joan and I walked through the neighborhood, I had pointed out slow-selling property, offering a self-righteous "Oops, I guess those people got a little greedy." Now I walked by those homes with far more empathy. We hadn't been greedy, had we? Maybe they weren't either. Walking down Peachtree Circle just made us wince, knowing that money was draining from our portfolio each month. "Why doesn't somebody buy our house?" Joan asked with a frustrated moan week after week. Sometimes we chose a different route to walk, just so we wouldn't have to deal with looking at the stale merchandise. But we knew why we were avoiding our old street, and that triggered depressing thoughts anyway.

After we moved, our home insurer forced us to take "vacant home insurance" at twice the price of our normal policy. That was both insult *and* injury. Just the name of it reminded us that the home was vacant—and we were spending more than $4,000 a year to insure a house that people rarely entered.

That the house wasn't selling was genuinely vexing. But the fastest way to heal any wound is through positive energy, and we are a glass-half-full group, so we focused on the pluses in our life. There were plenty.

For one thing, our real estate agent, Sally George, changed companies, which gave us the hope of reinvigoration for the house sale. Far more significantly, after a year of working her tail off to make a deal happen, she announced to us one day that she had decided to donate tens of thousands of dollars to our project. There were high-fives all around when Joan and I told the kids. We had another heartwarming endorsement.

Beyond that, we were intrigued with the transition to our new home. Until now, living in half had been mostly theory: What would we miss? Would our space feel squeezed or sacrificial? Now we were beginning to experience what half-life could be, with Joseph, Joan, and I in the upstairs bedrooms and Hannah on the lower level in what she called her lair.

It would be the best move we ever made. Not the best house, but the best move.

Our home on Walker Terrace looks vanilla from the outside, but the interior feels a bit like it was designed by M. C. Escher. I can't tell you how it got this way—maybe it's the result of a few renovations—but the place has five different sets of steps inside (not including those to the attic). As a result, it's common for one of us to yell to another, "What level are you on?" The living room, dining room, and kitchen are on one floor, but you have to either climb seven stairs or descend five to reach a toilet. Hannah's room is down still another staircase. The TV room looks like someone cross-bred a ski lodge with an auto mechanic's bay; the eleven-foot-high sloping wood-paneled ceiling leads into floor-to-ceiling windows with metal muntins.

Offbeat design or not, we began to live more tightly, and as a result more cohesively. For instance, in our old house the Ping-Pong table was virtually buried in the little-used basement; here, since there was no place else to put it, we stuck the table in the walkway to that ski lodge/car care TV room. Now that Ping-Pong was front and center, we began playing more. Usually Joseph grabbed a paddle first, then held his backswing for the exact moment when Joan, Hannah, or I could pick up the other paddle and prepare to return his serve. The kids' teenaged friends fit right in; with more players, we could expand the game to round robin, with all of us racing around the table, hitting a shot, then leaving the paddle for the next player. Some nights a dozen of us played for an hour, usually with lots of laughter.

Our piano moved from a back room at the old house to the living room of the Walker Terrace place. "Hey, Joe, get your guitar, and let's play a duet," Hannah would yell. Then she would play the only song she knew, her cousin Alex's "Hourglass," recorded by his band, Red Goodbye. Hannah would repeat the notes over and over as Joseph improvised a guitar line. Then they'd film themselves and post the video for Alex on Facebook. It was another small bonding moment in our little community.

That's not to say the downsizing didn't pinch.

One big loss was natural light, particularly in the kitchen. On Peachtree Circle, two sets of French doors opened to a balcony and the wooded back yard. Between that wall of windows and others on two sides of the room, sunshine streamed in, bouncing off the countertops and island. Here on Walker Terrace, our kitchen had three standard-size windows that looked out over a shared six-foot-wide driveway and our neighbor's light-shielding house. It was uncomfortable being in the room without the overhead fixture on.

Our pots and pans fit fine into the kitchen cabinets, but that was about the extent of the space. Counters felt cluttered, with limited working area. We couldn't open the silverware drawer without closing the dishwasher, which made unloading clean forks and knives a two-step job. The pantry was so narrow that the dog food took up a disproportionate share of space on the floor; extra paper towel rolls and cans of Coke Zero got moved to the unfinished basement.

Even though we had thrown away a lot and given so much to Goodwill, storage instantly became a badly cut jigsaw puzzle. Joan's dresses turned into orphans when the master bedroom lacked a closet tall enough to hold them. Our treadmill had to be exiled to the unheated garage. The coat closet was one third the size of our old one, and in the back of the house, far from any door.

None of this, of course, was much more than a minor hassle, a problem to be worked around. It was a bit like going from a weekend at the Four Seasons to a stay at a Hampton Inn. There was nothing wrong with the new property; it just called for an adjustment of mindset. And of course the thought of complaining about it to anyone would have been ludicrous, especially when we thought about those who were to receive our funds. We had chosen this path consciously and purposefully (if not a bit impetuously).

When Joan's parents came to visit, we made Joseph vacate his room and sleep on the TV room couch. He quickly learned that when he complained, it prompted a lecture from Joan or me about our childhoods, explaining how we had grown up in a one-and-a-half-bathroom house, shared a shower, blah blah blah. The first time he listened. The second time he rolled his eyes. Then he stopped mentioning his minor hardship.

Beyond that, though, our kids barely noticed any drawbacks. In fact, it began to bug Joan that Hannah and Joseph seemed oblivious of any downsizing inconveniences, regardless of how minor they were.

One night, relaxing over a juice glass of Shiraz about two weeks after our move, Joan waited until the kids had left the room. "I'm a little worried," she confided to me. "I wonder if this feels sacrificial enough for the kids. We have so much space here for everything they want to do. Shouldn't they be missing something more badly?" Joan's point was that we all should have been feeling some diminishment, a transfer from us to others; but it wasn't quite there, certainly for the kids.

She didn't expect an answer to her rhetorical question. But I laughed. "We just subtracted more than three thousand square feet from our lives," I replied, and then preemptively added, "and no, we're not downsizing again." Joan's face dropped into a disappointed frown, and it took me a few seconds to realize that it was her fake upset face.

But it was a reflection of how little sacrifice we felt. In fact, when we paused to consider our transition, we struggled to find anything major we missed from the larger space. For a back yard, we now used a nearby public park, where Joseph practiced kicking footballs and hitting baseballs. We parked on the street instead of on the big curving driveway. I certainly didn't miss anything about the bigger lawn or the additional home maintenance. In total, the subtractions in this equation didn't put us anywhere near zero.

A few days after settling in, we were greeted by more good news. Hannah and Joseph were home from school and Joan was working late to complete some yearbook pages when she called my cell. "Can you get H and J? I want to tell you all something." She had an edge to her voice and I asked what was up, but Joan insisted that the three of us hear the news at the same time; sensing my worry, she soothed me with a quick "It's nothing bad." So I called the kids into the hallway, propped my phone on top of the buffet, and pushed the speakerphone button. "Ready. We're all here," I announced.

"Joseph won!" Joan declared. "I just got off the phone with Coldwell Banker and Scholastic. His movie got the grand prize—two thousand bucks! Can you believe it?" Hannah, Joseph, and I didn't hear the last question; we were too busy screaming. "Oh yeah, oh yeah," Joseph said through an enormous grin.

When we settled down, Joan had a couple of housekeeping items to attend to. For instance, Scholastic wanted to donate books to Joseph's school, but the Westminster library already boasts one of the nation's largest children's book collections, so we decided to find a needier school. The company also wanted to throw a pizza party for his class, but Joseph wanted none of the attention that would bring at school, so he asked Joan to say no.

By the time Joan got home an hour later, Joseph had prepared his strategy for spending the two thousand dollars. Top on the list was a thousand dollars for a new guitar. Another two hundred would be dedicated to music accessories, and the remaining eight hundred would be set aside for savings. He stood back hopefully as Joan and I considered his proposal, handwritten on lined notebook paper.

"Wait a minute," I said. "Nothing to the Hunger Project? Isn't there some responsibility to give some to them? Like, how about half?"

Joseph remained quiet, but Hannah quickly interjected, "He won the prize. I think Joe should decide where the money goes."

Joan surprised me. "None of us has contributed individual money to this," she said. "We're using our collective funds, the amount we're harvesting from the house sale. I don't think this should go into the Hunger Project's pile."

I had expected more support from Joan and Hannah. Without it, I decided not to push, and after a bit more discussion Joseph had the green light to buy a guitar. The quid pro quo: he had to earmark eight hundred dollars for his college fund, and I agreed to invest it for him.

Soon after, we solidified our commitment to the Hunger Project. After a series of discussions with John Coonrod, the organization's chief operating officer, we agreed to fund the construction of two epicenters in Africa. Each epicenter, serving up to a dozen villages, typically features a meeting hall, a bank for microloans, a food storage facility, and a health center, complete with a small residence for a nurse. Each center costs $400,000 to construct and to fund the five years of programs that help the villagers become more self-reliant, healthier, and more empowered.

We locked in to build two epicenters, at a total cost of $800,000, one starting that year and one starting the next, each lasting five years from the start. Now the only question was where in Africa we would work.

Through our family research, we had already considered that question. It may sound odd, but we simply didn't care much. After all, we reasoned, when one in every six people on the planet was living on less than a dollar a day, we didn't have to look hard to find people in need.

John had a proposal for us. "I know you want to work in Africa," he said in a Skype call. "How would you feel about Ghana?" The Hunger Project, he explained, had begun a huge push in the poverty-stricken Eastern Region of the country, bankrolled by a New York foundation headed by the hedge-fund manager Julian Robertson. The foundation was willing to match our pledge, helping to build four epicenters instead of two and reaching some forty thousand villagers.

"Sounds good to us," Joan said, after glancing at the rest of us and seeing no objection. "Ghana it is."

We weren't off the call for more than a second or two when I voiced the question on all of our minds: "Where on earth is Ghana?" Hannah was ahead of me, already launching her Google search to begin our study of this West African nation bordering the Atlantic Ocean.

We can help, we said to one another. *We'll invest in the villagers of Ghana.*

One March day my friend Amy Unell from the *Today* show e-mailed to ask how I was doing. Three and a half years earlier, the premiere issue of my company's magazine had come across her desk. Amy took it home, read it, and the next day called me from NBC's Burbank offices to ask who we were and to rave about our perspective on business and life. She and I instantly bonded; we were kindred spir-

HANNAH'S TAKE

Experiencing the Lives of Others

A MAJOR PROBLEM OF MOTIVATION IS THAT MOST PEOPLE cannot even begin to feel what people with less means go through every day. Many people feel pity for people less fortunate than themselves. But the big leap is from pity to honest understanding. For me, a very important step in our project was to look at my life compared to others'.

Have you ever heard the old Indian folktale of the blind men and the elephant? In the story, a group of blind men touch an elephant and then describe what they are feeling. One rubs the tail and thinks the elephant is like a rope; others compare the parts to a wall or a snake. The point of the fable is that people see only a small portion of reality. We live in a narrow world, and it's so important to see things from different perspectives.

To really experience the sensation of hunger, our family completed the 30 Hour Famine, a fast of a little longer than a day that can easily be done with your family or with a school or religious group. This exercise helps you experience what someone who may not eat for a day goes through frequently. (You can find out more about this project, sponsored by World Vision, at www.30hourfamine.org.) When I tried this activity, I found that all I thought about was food. I tried to keep my mind busy with movies and phone conversations, and I can't even imagine not having distractions like those (as the truly hungry often don't). There are good activities on the 30 Hour Famine website that not only keep your mind busy but also raise money for hunger relief.

If hunger isn't your interest, here are a few others:

POVERTY: In 2007, Ted Kulongoski, the governor of Oregon, and many members of Congress decided to try the Food Stamp Challenge, attempting to feed themselves on what the average food-stamp recipient gets. What they found is that having only twenty-one dollars per week to spend on food makes healthy eating impossible. Imagine going to the grocery store every day and having a budget of only three dollars. The first thing you'd give up is fruits and vegetables and meat or fish, because they're the most expensive. After taking on the Food Stamp Challenge, Congress-woman Barbara Lee said, "It's hard to concentrate for any length of time on anything except food. I don't know how people with no money for decent meals do anything — study, work, exercise, read, have fun, etc. It's all about just making it through the day." I know how she felt.

WATER: A large problem that we saw when we visited Ghana was how hard it was to get clean water. People were forced to walk miles to get it. Want to try it? Turn off your main water source at your home and make a deal with a neighbor three blocks away to let you use his or her water for two days. Carry that water can back to your house — no driving! Remember, each gallon of water weighs more than eight pounds, and toilets typically take three gallons. At least you'll be strong by the end.

HOMELESSNESS: According to a 2007 study, there are nearly 754,000 homeless people in the United States at any time, nearly half of them living on the streets. (Many homeless groups think that number is way low.) How does that feel? Try it by sleeping with your family in a cardboard box out in your yard or inside your garage. You might add to the experience by only using public restrooms, not having the chance to wash your clothes, and not using your cell phone. My guess is you'll find this much tougher than camping trips.

its looking to live more purposefully, me through the magazine and Amy through TV stories that often ran as part of her network's "Making a Difference" series.

My reply to her e-mail was unexceptional: I described a friend's environmental software company, which I was helping, and some consulting offers I had gotten. I've found that when people ask, "What are you doing now?" (or the cocktail party standard "What do you do?"), they are almost always wondering about your professional life. People rarely answer "What do you do?" with "I coach youth hockey and jog three mornings a week."

But at this point my personal life was a lot more interesting than my work and Amy was a friend, so I added a link to Joseph's movie.

A few days later, Amy e-mailed again. This time the subject line was "Preguntas." She started with her trademark "Yo Kev" opening and praised Hannah's idea with a few exclamation-point-punctuated compliments. But then she added a half dozen questions—how did we decide to work in Africa, were we planning to travel, and so forth. *Odd,* I thought; this had quickly gone beyond a friendly chat. I answered her queries, then added a question of my own: Are you asking because you think it's a story?

Amy confessed immediately. She and the correspondent John Larson were interested in doing a piece about our project for *Today.* They thought the "Making a Difference" segment would match our concept nicely.

Suddenly we had a dilemma. Our family had shut down public discussion of our project; Joan's "I'm tired of feeling like a weirdo" rant from nearly a year earlier was still resonating. "I don't think I want to do this," Joan reiterated as we gathered at dinner that night.

Hannah was aghast. "Are you kidding, Mom? It's the *Today* show. A lot of my friends watch that."

Joseph agreed. "Yeah, so many people see the *Today* show, maybe one of them will buy our house."

For the next ten minutes we talked about the pros and cons of coming out from behind our veil of silence. I suggested that since our project was so beneficial for our family, it might be a plus for others to hear our story. Hannah focused on a different type of inspiration: "I think it could get other families to do something good. Maybe they'll get pumped up about helping in the world," she said.

After a few minutes Joan relaxed her stance, acknowledging that Joseph's movie had taught us how to tell our story less clumsily. And finally she put forward a proposal. "I would agree to being more open about this," she began, formulating the structure as she spoke. "But any publicity would need to have three elements. It would first have to reach people who might buy the house—in other words, help us finance the project. Second, it would hopefully inspire others, and third, we would name the Hunger Project, bringing more awareness and money to the organization." With no significant objection from the kids or me, we signed on to those conditions.

A few weeks later John Coonrod called to ask about the Hunger Project's annual meeting, to be held in New York in April. Would Hannah speak? he wondered. "Nothing too elaborate—just a few words on why the family chose to invest with us. It's all friends in that room, maybe a hundred people, our board, investors, people like that."

Friends or not, Hannah went into instant panic.

I could see why. In some ways, school curriculums drive me crazy. I have long thought that schools spend too much time teaching subjects that few students will ever use down the road (chemistry and trigonometry, for instance). But most kids never learn enough about how to thrive in the real world. Why doesn't everyone have to take classes in leadership? After all, at some point every person will use those skills, whether in a business setting, running a Little League team, or heading up a community-pool group. No one should graduate without learning at least the basics of how to communicate with and motivate others.

Hannah could have used a course in public speaking. Her total number of presentations for the year was two, both announcements to the school about social events. And within a couple of days the pressure got turned up even higher: *Today* decided that it wanted to send a crew to New York to film Hannah's Hunger Project speech. Forget about learning to walk before she ran. Hannah was in full sprint.

Hannah has many great traits in life, but planning isn't one of them. She waited until we were traveling to New York that April weekend to begin thinking through her remarks and instantly slipped into lack-of-confidence mode. "I have no idea what to say," she announced.

"They just want to know why we chose the Hunger Project," I offered flippantly.

But Hannah's nerves made her testy. "Well, duh, Dad. Of

course I know that. I just don't know how to say it," she snapped back.

Things calmed down as we checked into our hotel, and for a while that evening we talked about the messages she could use. Hannah jotted down a few notes but opted for an early bedtime.

The next morning was consumed with compensating for Joseph's packing snafus. He had left his black dress shoes at home, and Joan insisted that well-worn Nikes were inappropriate with a navy blazer and tie, so our first stop was a local shoe store, for a new pair of lace-ups. While we were there, Joseph sheepishly confessed that he'd left his white dress shirt back in Atlanta too; that triggered a trip to Filene's Basement for a replacement.

With the haberdashery part of our morning finished, we walked to the Juan Valdez Café, on Manhattan's East Side. There, at a corner table, over muffins, Colombian coffee, and milk, Joan, Joseph, and I acted as sounding boards for Hannah's presentation. "Thank your host first. Don't forget to look up at your audience," Joan reminded her. "And do the speech slowly. It always sounds faster to other people than it does to you." Hannah wrote feverishly on note cards, then rehearsed as we gently critiqued her phrases and delivery.

We spent the rest of the day visiting friends and browsing in the Union Square farmers' market. In one part of the park, for a reason that never became apparent to us, an eccentric group of twentysomethings was offering free hugs to passersby. Hannah got four of them.

At 7 P.M. we arrived at the top floor of the Doubletree

Hotel on Lexington Avenue and entered Hannah Salwen's Theater of Terror.

When we walked into the cocktail party portion of the board dinner, we found the NBC crew already there, fully armed with cameras, lights, and a none-too-subtle boom mike. "Just wander around the way you would at any party," the producer told us. "Pretend we're not here." Um, right.

As if the kids didn't feel self-conscious enough with a camera crew trailing them, NBC had asked Joseph to document the event in his "award-winning video style." So he was filming Hannah with his JVC camcorder, and NBC was alternately filming Hannah and filming Joseph filming Hannah.

Beyond that, our kids were the youngest people at the function by two decades. Hannah, already worried about her speech, worked the room with a forced smile on her face, introducing herself to others—sometimes two or three times by mistake. At one point she walked up to a woman wearing a blue business suit and offered her standard perky "Hi, I'm Hannah." The woman answered, "Yes, we've met." A minute later Hannah walked past me, mumbling, "That was so unbelievably awkward!"

But when the evening transitioned from cocktail hour to dinnertime, we found that the Hunger Project had been smart; they had placed Hannah next to Dr. Speciosa Wandira. They couldn't have chosen a more relaxing dinner partner. Speciosa, as she insisted on being called, was the first woman elected vice president of Uganda during the post–Idi Amin era; that made her the highest-ranking female official in Africa. Now she was working on a doctorate at

Harvard University's School of Public Health, and she was eager to return to Uganda to continue to better her country. She was on the Hunger Project's international board of directors.

Although she has such impressive professional achievements, Speciosa's primary character trait is warmth, reflected in her winning smile. She was curious, eager to chat. "So, why are you here?" she asked Hannah, putting her hand lightly on Hannah's shoulder, just above the cream-colored strapless dress.

Despite the tension of the event, Hannah's reply was relaxed and focused. Forget the filming of Joseph's movie in the living room, with its muddled message. This time Hannah never once looked over at me and Joan for intervention or clarity. She told Speciosa our family story, explaining how we had decided to work in Africa, how the Hunger Project's values matched ours, how our worksheet process worked.

Speciosa beamed as Hannah talked, and her grin got even larger when she learned that Hannah had been the trigger for the project. "Oh, Hannah, you must come work with us in Uganda too," she said. "You will *love* our country, just *love* it."

The dinner was a high-end buffet. Hannah put enough food on her plate to appear polite, then pushed around her chicken and ate a roll; then she took the bread off my plate as well. It was a bun-and-butter meal.

Finally Jill Lester, who had just become the CEO of the Hunger Project following Joan Holmes's retirement, arrived at the lectern. In a lilting Australian accent, she spoke for several minutes about what she had learned during a brief inaugural trip to Bangladesh, India, and Africa. Next to me, Hannah had tuned out, tensely waiting for her own performance, just minutes away. And soon Jill introduced her.

Hannah strode to the center of the room and positioned herself behind the pair of microphones, one that would amplify her in the room, the other for the *Today* show's video sound. Back at the hotel, she had toiled for more than half an hour straightening her hair, getting her makeup right, and putting on a simple silver necklace with the peace symbol she loved.

As Hannah settled in, I glanced at the audience seated in groups of ten around white tablecloth–covered tables. This was a truly international group, with saris and dashikis scattered among the suits and dresses and the globe's complete range of skin colors. There seemed to be a mixture of surprise and expectation in their faces as they watched a fifteen-year-old step before them. Coffee cups were placed down gently in saucers; conversations became muted. What would this girl tell us?

Hannah's opening line triggered an instant interruption. "Thank you, Ms. Lester, I'm really happy to be here," Hannah said, following Joan's "thank your host" advice.

"Just Jill will be fine," the CEO interjected, in an effort to be warm. The audience laughed. Luckily, so did Hannah, who resumed her remarks without a hitch. She quickly explained our family's decision to downsize and "donate half the sales price to help end hunger in Africa. So we researched dozens of organizations to see who would do the most good with our money . . ."

I winked at Joan as Hannah worked her way through our story, describing our trip to New York to interview the finalists and our selection of the Hunger Project. Heads were nodding in the audience. "We loved the fact that the Hunger Project, more than any other organization we met with, believes in the human spirit," she told the audience. *And no one,* I said to myself, *believes in the human spirit more than Hannah does.*

As Hannah finished with the line "I love what the Hunger Project is doing and I'm proud to be working side by side with them," her body relaxed; her task was done. She walked back to our table to warm applause and sat down. I patted her on the thigh; her new best friend, Speciosa, put her arm around Hannah and they gave each other a side hug.

Just over an hour later we were back in our hotel, off-camera at last. None of us wanted to stay late at the dinner, and none of us wanted to go out. It was nine-thirty and the stress of the day had taken its toll. New York might be the city that never sleeps, but we wanted to be alone and out of sight. We stripped off our formal clothes, Joan and I hanging ours up and the kids tossing theirs on chairs. Then we climbed into bed and all watched *Dumb & Dumber,* the slapstick movie starring Jim Carrey and Jeff Daniels. We needed the mindless relief.

The next morning we flew home.

When we returned to Atlanta, we prepared for the second half of the *Today* shoot. Amy and John Larson had decided they wanted on-the-ground color, so we agreed to meet for breakfast at our old haunt the Atlanta Diner. Walking in that morning, I noticed that someone—possibly a drunk patron from the bar next door—had broken off the arm of the ceramic waiter holding the chalked list of specials.

For an hour all four of us sat on one side of the table, like a sitcom family, answering John's questions as he tried to coax out just the right sound bites for the piece. We all tried to eat as politely as we could, not to talk with our mouths full of French toast, not to be cowed by the bright lights and lapel microphones. But there just wasn't any way to be ourselves in this environment.

I've found that there's an interesting facet to television interviews: it's easy to know when you're doing poorly, with plenty of stumbles, ums, and ers. But it's harder to know when you're doing well, in part because facial expressions can so often negate good phrasing.

One thing Hannah knew for sure: she was terrified, backsliding into run-on-sentence mode. That's the way it is with teens, I guess, nailing it one night (as at the Hunger Project speech and with Speciosa) and being awkward and uncomfortable the next.

At one point John asked her to describe an epicenter, the L-shaped central building of a Hunger Project program. "Well, um, it's got a bank and a school and, um—what's in there again?" John tried to relax her and then offered, "Let's try that again. Hannah, what's an epicenter?" Another stumble-filled reply. On the fourth try Hannah hit bottom: "Well, it's a school and a library and . . . oh, crap." We all burst into laughter, and John good-naturedly said she could give it another shot later.

From the diner we headed to the Atlanta Community

Food Bank for visuals of Hannah doing the volunteer work that had gotten her started on the journey that culminated with the house sale. Food bank staffers, despite their surprise at this impromptu visit from a national TV show, genially squeezed Hannah in among red-T-shirted volunteers from Bank of America to sort cans and other packages of food. But that didn't produce the right cinematic effect, so the cameraman rearranged people and objects further.

Hannah worked hard to play along. "This is Spaghetti-Os," she said, placing the can into a cardboard box. But her matter-of-fact commentary masked her real feelings, a combination of embarrassment at the public filming and, far worse, anxiety over her belief that she was stomping on others' volunteer experience. That was a real sin.

A few minutes later *Today's* cameras caught Hannah dropping a jar of relish onto the concrete floor, where it shattered and spilled gooey pickle product at her feet. The producers were kind enough to leave that out of the edited version.

I understood what the NBC team was looking for. In my decades as a journalist, I had done thousands of interviews, hunting for just the right quote, the perfect story to illustrate a point. It can be a struggle to craft a story arc, and behind the scenes things can look a bit like a sausage factory; the viewer doesn't really see what's in there, and probably doesn't want to. Now I suddenly realized how stressful it was to have the questions aimed at me, to fret over misspeaking, to want each sentence to contain just the right context. Despite camera angles, sound bites, and careful editing, no one could truly capture our family's dynamic or motivations in a less-than-three-minute video piece. Journalism is two-dimensional storytelling in a 3D world.

Next we headed for Café 458, so that Hannah could show how she served the homeless men and women there. Again, since she wasn't expected, other volunteers were already doing the work. But at the urging of the TV crew, Hannah hunted for plates to carry from the kitchen, sweet tea to pour, and dishes to clean. From the center of the room, Hannah didn't miss the faces of the volunteers; they were far from amused by the imposition.

We wrapped up the shoot in the early afternoon, filming at both our old house and our new one. But as the NBC crew shot scenes at Peachtree Circle, I felt a swell of an emotion I had never anticipated: I was *angry* at this house—this unsold, petulant, progress-blocking structure. It was that irrational kind of slow-boil anger, the kind you feel when a relationship has soured, when all the things you once loved in the other person have evaporated. All I could see was the house's warts. I detected every stain on the walls, every chip in the furniture, every crack in the driveway. Dust or cobwebs leapt out at me as untidy reminders of a house unoccupied.

As the *Today* cameraman walked through the spacious hallways filming the coffered ceilings and the gold-leaf paint, my vision was darker, of burned-out light bulbs and broken window sashes. "I can't stand this place," I grumbled, jiggling the seemingly always-running toilet in the downstairs bathroom. It certainly wasn't home anymore, just a stale old piece of property.

As our family and the NBC crew headed over to the hastily cleaned-up Walker Terrace house, my emotional pulse shifted. Joan and I had scrambled the day before to hang a few pieces of art and wash the tablecloth covering the rectangular white plastic folding table that served as our dining room furniture. Our front walk and shared driveway had been swept clean.

As we pulled up to the curb, I realized that this was our house now, the new relationship. It wasn't just *where* we lived but a reflection of *how* we lived—closer, more tightly. There were plenty of warts here, I knew, but they didn't matter nearly as much as the ones at the old house. We saw the good in this place. This house was smaller, but our world was bigger.

HANNAH'S TAKE

The Test Drive

WE ALL HAVE DIFFERENT INTERESTS. NOT EVERYONE IS GOOD with kids, the seriously ill, or the homeless. You might prefer to go to a nursing home to play bingo with the residents. My point is that service is not one-size-fits-all; it helps to find something you love. But how?

When I was getting started, I considered a bunch of volunteer opportunities. Some were easy to eliminate. A lot of my friends thought it would be cool to work at the Humane Society or to help kids through therapeutic horseback riding. But since I'm afraid of both dogs and horses, they weren't for me. I'd love to be a ski guide for the blind, but I definitely don't ski well enough to do something like that. Others were worth trying out. I tested senior-center visits, going a few times with my family to sing on Thanksgiving or play bingo on a Sunday morning. It wasn't a great fit for me. I'm not great with the elderly and often don't feel comfortable around them.

But I realized that I liked getting involved with the homeless and those living in poverty by going to Café 458 and the Central Night Shelter. I worked at the Atlanta Community Food Bank, boxing and weighing foods to be shipped to soup kitchens and food pantries. When I realized that I liked one kind of service more than the others, I started volunteering more often.

Do the same. Try different categories of service. Figuring out your talents will help you realize what sort of volunteering work you want to get more deeply involved with.

Activity

Pick three volunteer opportunities you can do as a family — for example, tutoring little children, volunteering at a soup kitchen, and planting trees with an environmental committee. (For ideas, a great site is www.handsonnetwork.org. Also, religious institutions regularly offer service activities.)

When you get home from volunteering, document your experience. Once you have completed your three activities, write down the elements you liked best about them. For instance, you might have enjoyed working outdoors or being with a large group of people or being directly involved with the folks you were helping. Then compare notes with your family to decide if those activities are the right ones or whether you should keep looking for ways to get more of the best elements. You definitely don't have to stop searching here, and you can keep sampling.

One last thing: try not to plan too many other things around your volunteer outing. Instead, leave yourselves a few hours afterward. Whenever our family does something good in the community, we reward ourselves by going out to IHOP or Dairy Queen. We talk about what we did while we scarf down a treat. It makes the whole experience more fun — plus it gives us time to chat.

7

What Do We Do?

— — — — - — — -

My father used to say, "You can spend a lot of time
making money. The tough time comes when you
have to give it away properly." How to give something
back, that's the tough part in life.

— Lee Iacocca

L AND HO AFRICA!" Hannah wrote in exuber-
ance in her journal. We dragged off the Delta jet
in Ghana's capital, Accra, our bodies stiff from
the ten-hour overnight flight from New York's Kennedy
Airport.

Our flight had been sold out. Apparently this is one of
Delta's most profitable routes; the seats were stuffed with
African and American businessmen, Ghanaians living in
America who were headed home to see family, and teenagers beginning mission trips with matching T-shirts proclaiming their service. One of the flight attendants was
wearing an African scarf over her airline uniform. "Oh,
you're just going to *love* Ghana," she told me as she handed
me the dinner tray.

Hannah, Joseph, Joan, and I were feeling a jumble of emotions: excitement, uncertainty, even mild fear. In some ways it felt to Joan and me like our wedding day, a situation where the months-long buildup takes you to a singular event. To the kids it was more like a last-inning, two-out baseball at-bat or the serve at game point in a volleyball match. We had worked long and hard for this moment. Now, 5,675 miles from home, we were as prepared as practice could make us.

But we couldn't sidestep our nagging questions. What if this journey was a flop? So many variables had become fused together in this melding of overseas travel and family philanthropy. At the surface were the creature-comfort issues: Would there be disgusting bugs and inedible food? Would our lodging be awful? Would we feel put off by the human conditions we encountered?

Much more critically, of course, this trip represented the first real yardstick of whether our huge family bet might go awry. This wasn't a safari or sightseeing; it was the incubator for whether our money would help grow a community.

The night before we left for Ghana, as we were finishing the packing, Joan stuffed dozens of Ben's Tick and Insect Repellent Wipes (with extra deet) into a black Eddie Bauer duffel bag. "No malaria for us, thank you very much," she said, laughing with a slight air of unease.

But her tone soon turned more serious as she let her doubt bubble up. I was folding some Nike golf shirts into my bag when her voice changed. "You know, lots of smart people have tried and failed to alleviate rural poverty," she said, her voice soft and tinged with concern. "It's really hard. And we only have one big house to sell—we won't get another shot at this. We can't learn and make it right the next time."

I started to reply but then recalled possibly the best piece of relationship advice I had ever received, from a family friend nearly three decades earlier: "Sometimes the other person doesn't actually need a reply, but instead just needs to get things said. Let her talk and just listen." As we stood in the bedroom packing, it was clear that Joan wasn't done. Her unease, she explained, went deeper than just money or time or effort, all real worries in their own right. She didn't want to fail in the biggest, most visible, most inter- connected project our family had ever taken on. "Kev, I so badly want our efforts to be rewarded," she said. "I don't want this to be a place where our kids learn the life lesson that even when you do the right thing, success sometimes eludes you. I want to save that for another time."

I walked around to her side of the bed and hugged her.

For her part, Hannah was toggling between tactical and emotional concerns. She harbored an oversized fear of throwing up, so she worried that foreign germs would in- vade her body. On a deeper level, she too felt the stirrings of uncertainty. A few weeks earlier, as we lay around the new house's TV room at one of our family meetings, we had marveled yet again at the amount of money that had been invested in Africa with scant results. Hannah, sitting with her legs propped up in the el of the sectional sofa, had pro- cessed the concept once more. But this time her face sud- denly turned cold, her eyes narrowing. "What happens if this doesn't work?" she wondered aloud. "I mean, what happens if we go back five years from now and nothing is different for the people we're trying to help?"

It was, of course, a question that Joan and I had considered before; we had simply been alive long enough to see decades of failed efforts to end poverty both in the United States and abroad. But coming from Hannah, it was a lightning bolt. Our daughter had turned a corner, recognizing the risks in what we were doing. This wasn't the "I want to make a difference in the world" Hannah; instead, it was more "What if we can't help change happen?" When I heard her question, my first reaction was pride: our daughter was growing out of naiveté. But that emotion mixed instantly with a touch of sadness that a little of her idealism might be slipping away. What was the hurry?

Joan offered comforting words, but her reply reflected what she and I knew: that in the end, success or failure would be dictated by many factors outside our control. "There's definitely a chance of that, Han. That's why we've done our process, learning what works and what doesn't. We've put our faith in the Hunger Project and the villagers together to get it right, and I think in the end that's the best we can do."

On the flight to Ghana, if Hannah was having doubts, she didn't express them. Freed from school requirements, she watched movie after movie through the night without a trace of guilt, until finally fatigue set in and she slumped against the window shade to drift off. Sitting behind me, Joan couldn't sleep, so she read West Africa travel guides, hoping to pick up nuggets of useful information.

Next to Joan, Joseph wrote a haiku in his journal:

Oh this plane I'm on,
Carry me to Africa,
For I wish to go.

A dozen rows back, our new friend John Coonrod filled in Sudoku puzzles and slept. When we had met at the airport, I had done a double-take when I realized that John was carrying only a backpack for a trip to Africa. He had a small digital camera, a book of expert Sudoku puzzles, and some obviously very resilient clothes. Talk about packing light. Now, as I glanced at him on the plane, he looked like a casual traveler off to see a relative for Thanksgiving. At the advice of a doctor, we had packed a medicine chest full of remedies for diarrhea, sleeplessness, yeast infections, and allergic reactions. By contrast, John had a sense of peace about this journey to remote, undeveloped villages that filled me first with calm (the guy knew what he was doing and I trusted that) and then with envy (how could I achieve that level of relaxation?).

When you get beyond the major cities of Europe and Asia, airports overseas can feel a bit like time traveling, back to an era before American terminals upgraded from smoky places selling warmed-over hot dogs to become today's shiny brand-name-laden concourses. When we left the plane, we descended an exterior metal staircase for the walk across the tarmac to the terminal. No jetways here, no flat-screen TVs blaring CNN. This was 1960s air travel, quainter and more utilitarian. We were in Africa! In Ghana, that place we'd had to scramble to locate on a map just six months earlier.

Why were we here? In Joseph's movie for the Coldwell Banker contest, he reflected our family's thinking up to that point with this line: "We are getting directly involved." But what did that actually mean? What were we to do halfway around the globe? How could we help? Simple questions, really, but the answers were far more complex than we had ever thought.

The easy way to start answering those questions is to look at what we *weren't* doing in Ghana. When we began our family project, we were convinced that we would be, in Joseph's term, "directly involved." We presumed that involvement would reflect what Westerners traditionally see as their role. We'd be digging wells or laying bricks or painting walls. We'd be working side by side with Africans, spending our money and our time catalyzing brighter futures for them. We'd be at the center of the action, the costars of this play.

But then we read and learned, and the conclusions were eye-opening, even shocking. Here's one: mission and service trips often have a negative long-term impact on the very people they are aiming to serve—not positive, not even neutral, but negative. It may be hard to believe that people of goodwill aspiring to help those in need can have a deleterious effect. But they do.

A Princeton University study showed that more than 1.6 million people go on mission trips in a typical year, spending an average of eight days. The total invested in these sojourns: $2.4 billion a year. But evidence is growing that the social impact can be a huge minus for the developing world.

Critics deride the trips as "religious tourism" for "vacation-aries." Often the activities undertaken by these groups are little more than make-work. The *Washington Post* noted that one Mexican church was painted six times by six different mission groups in a single summer.

As ludicrous as repainting freshly painted walls can be for the travelers, the locals often are the real losers. Unless service trips empower local people in some important way, they do little but help to foster dependence. In some ways it's human nature fighting against itself. Few of us can resist a gift, even when it keeps us from enhancing our fundamental abilities.

Take this example from Bob Lupton, the president of FCS Urban Ministries, a community development program in Atlanta. In a recent newsletter, Lupton told the story of his church's mission trip to a rural Honduran village.

> The remote peasant community needed water. The obvious solution: Dig them a well. There was great celebration when the first water was pumped to the surface and villagers filled their jugs with cold, pure water. But when our missioners returned the following year the pump was idle and locals were again carrying water from a distant supply. We repaired the pump. But by the time we returned the following year it had broken down again. This happened repeatedly year after year. The village simply waited until their benefactors returned.

Lupton also spoke with Juan Ulloa, who runs a microloan program in Nicaragua. Mission trip after mission trip took

Nicaraguans gifts of clothing and dozens of willing hands to build wells. Finally the frustrated Ulloa explained that there were entire sections of the country where his lending officers couldn't make any loans at all: "People say, 'Why should we borrow money when the churches give it to us?' . . . They're turning my people into beggars!"

That concept terrified our family. We certainly didn't want to turn anyone into a beggar. We already knew that the handout approach didn't work; at the macro level, the Western world's $2.3 trillion flop in aid over the past five decades had proved that with crystal clarity. Now, after learning about the problems of mission trips, we realized that results might not be any better at the micro level.

But where did that leave us? Was there a role beyond writing checks each year? Our family had always defined ourselves as doers, not watchers. What would we *do?* "Maybe we can read with the kids in the villages," Hannah suggested. "I could teach them how to play kickball," Joseph offered.

Our choice to partner with the Hunger Project reflected our view that Africans should be the authors of their own future. Surely, we figured, the team there would have the answers. So, the week before July Fourth, just after we got our tetanus, typhoid, yellow fever, and hepatitis A shots and began taking our malaria medicine, Joan called John Coonrod for answers.

"Okay, John," Joan began. "What are we going to be doing in Ghana, anyway? How can we best help?"

Just the way she asked the question reflected how seriously we wanted to take our responsibility. We had no interest in dictating the terms of this relationship; we recoiled at the concept of coming off as superior to "those poor people." We accepted that we didn't have all the answers; at least we were smart enough to see that.

John's reply set the parameters narrowly. "Just support their work. Show the villagers that you've come all the way from the U.S. to stand behind them. Let them show off their accomplishments."

"Anything else?" Joan pressed him, taking notes, her left hand scribbling on the back of a piece of junk mail.

"Nope, that's it, really. You're likely to be asked by chiefs to help fund other things, like a school. Even if you're tempted, don't promise more money or a shipment of clothing. And definitely don't bring gifts."

No gifts? That was a shock. We had planned to take T-shirts or books or shoes or something with us. Many of our friends had asked what kind of supplies to gather for us to take along and give away.

"That's all?" Hannah, Joseph, and I exclaimed together when Joan told us what she had learned over dinner that evening. "That seems weird, like we're not doing anything," Joseph added. Joan confided to me later that she harbored similar concerns about the visit-and-support plan. But she wasn't about to reveal any of that apprehensiveness here. Instead she explained that she trusted the Hunger Project's methodology and she urged us to do the same.

"Let's just see how it plays out," she told us, and we let it lie there.

Actually, after talking with a neighbor who had traveled extensively in developing nations, Joan decided to di-

verge slightly from John's strategy. She searched her computer files for a family photo, one of the four of us standing
in the living room of the Peachtree Circle house, and had
a hundred copies printed at Costco. She planned to give
them out as a gesture of friendship in the villages, exchanging our photo for pictures we would take of people we met.
When we rendezvoused with John at Kennedy Airport for
our flight to Accra, he concurred with Joan's photo idea. It
would be seen as friendly and giving in the right way, he
told her.

John was a veteran. Trained as a plasma physicist at
Berkeley in the 1970s, he had moved east to work on a
Princeton fusion-energy project trying to find a cheap solution to the world's electricity problems. The theory was
that inexpensive energy could be used to desalinate water, which could then be used to irrigate the Sahara des-
ert and feed Africa. But after six years of research, the
idea simply didn't work the way John had hoped. Fusion
wouldn't be an answer to world hunger issues for at least a
century.

By that time John had gotten to know Joan Holmes and
her nascent Hunger Project. He loved what was starting to
be called the human potential movement—the belief that
people could take charge of their destinies instead of waiting for external forces to help them. Just a few years earlier,
John had been heavily involved in the anti–Vietnam War
movement, showing him that if enough individuals chose
to make their voices heard, significant change was possible.
Now he wondered how far individuals' actions could move
the world. He believed deeply in the Hunger Project's vi-

sion of ending world poverty through empowerment and self-reliance. When Joan Holmes offered him a chance to join the organization, even with a 50 percent pay cut, he jumped at the chance.

John described his life transition to me in a conference room at the Hunger Project's Union Square office, stopping at one point to ask me a seemingly oddball question. "Have you read *War and Peace*?" he posed, looking across the table. I confessed that I hadn't, so John continued. "In nineteenth-century Europe, there was this 'great man' theory. In short, it was the belief that people like Napoleon were saviors and that great men made history. But Tolstoy believed just the opposite: that history makes these men great; they are puppets, and it is millions of small decisions made by everyday people that make up the great movements of history. Those movements of history call forth the Napoleons when they need them and throw them away when they are done with them."

Now John was rolling, adding his own perspective to Tolstoy's. "The decisions being made by the peaceful individual make up these great moments in history, and you can sure see that in the antiwar movement. When I was first in it, there was a handful of us and we were considered totally weird. Within seven or eight months there were moratorium marches attended by half a million people and the slogan was 'When grandmothers in tennis shoes join antiwar marches, Nixon knew the war had to be ended, that it was over.' We didn't call it the tipping point then, but it would have been if the term had existed."

In turn, the Hunger Project's goal became to build a

worldwide movement aware of the injustice of so many humans struggling with persistent hunger. That awareness would be the first step to solving the problem.

Thirty-plus years later at the organization, John remains one of the most passionate individuals I have ever encountered. He met his wife, Carol, at the Hunger Project. Having no kids and a relatively low mortgage payment, he and Carol decided to donate their excess cash to the organization. It got to be such a habit that one day John and Carol looked up and realized that they were the largest donors to the Hunger Project in New York, having given more than $500,000 over the years. When I looked shocked that two employees of a nonprofit group were able to be that generous, John just laughed. "I guess it proves I'm not a very good fundraiser if I couldn't get anyone to top us," he said with a wide grin. But then he got serious. "Between the two of us, we were giving back half our take-home pay."

"Don't you feel you're giving up a lot?" I asked him.

"No. What did I give up?" John asked, pointing out the conference room window to the twenty-seven-story brick building where he and Carol had been able to buy their apartment inexpensively seventeen years earlier. "I always wanted complete financial freedom and happiness, and I am thrilled we can give our money away. I don't want to be a hippie about this, but there is a voluntary simplicity that is not a sacrifice but a choice of freedom."

What John was saying, of course, is that without the need to accumulate, he felt less stress than others. He didn't long for what others possessed, even in New York, a city obsessed with the likes of Donald Trump's opulence and celebrities' excesses. He refused to get aboard the treadmill we had hopped on earlier in our lives.

Without even looking, I had stumbled across someone who was already living the power of half, and who had been doing so for *decades*. Neither John nor Carol was a flake. They didn't give because they felt guilty about having money. They just lived a life that made them happy through generosity and a sense of community. As I listened to John describing his life, I wondered what I might have thought of him a few years earlier, in the heart of our accumulation years. Would I have understood him? Could I have been open-minded enough not to dismiss him as a nutty idealist?

As I sat at the table in that Manhattan office, my mind leapt to the father of one of Joseph's baseball buddies. On ski vacations in Colorado, this man hires four different instructors, one for each member of his family. I thought about other friends for whom the old bumper sticker *Whoever dies with the most toys wins* could apply. Would they "get" John Coonrod?

To complete the thought in his conversation with me, John circled back to the villages where he has spent so much of his life. "I would say the most generous people and the people who have taught me most about money are villagers. If you walked in with your level of income and you needed food, water, or a place to stay, a villager wouldn't hesitate to give it to you. And then, if you protested, they would say, 'Oh, no, are you kidding? You would do the same for me in your country.' They cannot conceive of our level of stinginess. Sharing is just the way it is in these villages—their generosity is their enormous strength."

In 1977, when John was volunteering for the Hunger Project, he read a research paper from the National Academy of Sciences that included the eye-catching phrase "If there is the political will in this country and abroad . . . it should be possible to overcome the worst aspects of widespread hunger and malnutrition within one generation." That fit perfectly with his view that a committed group of impassioned individuals could create positive change. So why not end hunger and poverty in twenty years?

Needless to say, that twenty years had long passed by the time our family met John. But he remained intractably optimistic.

"Do you ever get down about what you haven't yet been able to accomplish—you know, missing that twenty-year goal?" I asked him.

He thought for a moment before he answered, rubbing his white beard. "When the Hunger Project started, there were only three democracies in Africa. Now there are forty-five. There were wars raging in dozens of countries. They are awful, but they are happening in less than a handful of countries. There were also no women's rights; now that is happening. Humanity does make slow, jerky progress. What keeps me in the game is this very palpable sense of being a part of history, and being on the right side of history."

John Coonrod, optimist and philosopher, was to be our travel companion for five days. (Our family would stay in Ghana for eight more.) Joan and I wondered, frankly, how this physicist/humanist with limited experience dealing with teenagers would relate to our kids and vice versa. We needn't have worried. Shortly after we landed in Accra, Hannah and Joseph decided that if we were going to travel together he needed a gangsta rap alias, so they christened him J-Coon. He laughed when he heard that playful riff on his name. "I guess it could have been worse," he said. As we traveled around the countryside, he dropped little lines about his "friends" the rappers Kanye West and P. Diddy. The forty-five-year gap between him and our kids narrowed with each laugh they shared.

Ghana is a nation of contrasts, and we began learning that just minutes after landing at Kotoka International Airport in Accra. Entering the terminal, we were greeted by a string of inviting touches. Black-and-white paper soccer balls hung from the ceiling alongside red, orange, and green bunting. AKWAABA. WELCOME TO GHANA, GATEWAY TO AFRICA, declared a blue sign with white lettering. Customs agents smiled with what we soon learned is typical Ghanaian friendliness.

But just a few steps farther, another sign, this one attached prominently to a wall, offered a starkly different, more cautionary worldview. It started hospitably enough: WELCOME. AKWAABA. GHANA WARMLY WELCOMES ALL VISITORS OF GOODWILL. Just beneath it, though, the tone turned harsh as we learned the billboard's real purpose: "Ghana does not welcome paedophiles and other sexual deviants. Indeed Ghana imposes extremely harsh penalties on such aberrant behaviour. If you are in Ghana for such activity, then for everybody's good, including your own, we suggest you go elsewhere."

We had read the Bradt travel guide to Ghana. We had learned about the sights, the foods, the transportation. We somehow never read about pedophilia in the book.

Still, as jarring as it was, the sign reflected the latest of many foul exploitations that have befallen this country. In the sixteenth century, the British, Portuguese, and Dutch traded gold out of Ghana. But it didn't take long for the Europeans to realize that they had an even more valuable export lying in their midst: people. In short order the most lucrative trade from Ghana became slaves. For centuries Ghanaians and their neighbors were forcibly rounded up and marched in chains to castles on the Gold Coast. From there, ships set sail for the New World packed with humans who would be owned by other humans. It's difficult to get a verifiable number, but some historians estimate that 6.3 million slaves were shipped from Ghana and the rest of West Africa in the 350 years of slave trading that ended in the mid-nineteenth century. Sickening.

The contrast in the airport between the upbeat soccer balls and the poster about dire exploitation carries through to Ghana at large. Ghana became the first colonial sub-Saharan African nation to gain independence, when the British withdrew in 1957. It is, relatively speaking, politically stable, with a democratically elected president and parliament. As a result of that stability and a decent supply of natural resources, the Ghanaian economy has been healthier than those of many of the continent's countries, with cash generated by gold, cocoa beans, and some tourism (mostly "roots" tours taken by African Americans). That said, the country has more than its share of abject poverty. According to the UN, nearly four out of five of Ghana's 24 million people live on less than two dollars a day. Half of those live on less than one dollar a day. For many, clothing consists of one or two simple cotton outfits that they wear for years. People often live in handmade huts smaller than the average American living room. With poor diet and limited medicine, average life expectancy is just fifty-nine years. Old age comes fast: even villagers in their forties look like senior citizens by our standards, with lined faces and worn teeth.

Given Ghana's history of being ravaged by outsiders, you might think the country would be reluctant to embrace visitors, especially white visitors. You might assume that distrust is rampant. But we couldn't help but feel warmed by the geniality of shopkeepers, craftsmen, farmers, and villagers. And it made me wonder: How painful must a nation's history be before its people stop embracing outsiders? Is there a threshold at which people just shut down to anyone but those they know? If there is, we never saw it in Ghana.

In fact, a few days into our trip, it occurred to me that Ghanaians are similar to what Hannah was pushing our family to be: unfailingly hopeful. They are aware of the potential pitfalls, but so eager to build a better future that the risk of doing nothing is far outstripped by the desire for improvement.

It's easy to see Africa from thousands of miles away as a

monolith, a single impoverished, needy entity rife with the corruption of Zimbabwe or the barbarism of the Sudan. But with our feet down in the continent, I wanted to understand how locals perceive their culture and people. "Describe the Ghanaian people for me," I asked many people I met. My favorite response came from a street artist in the central town of Kumasi. Referring to the aggressive, hardball nature of the country's neighbor a couple hundred miles to the east, his response was blunt but delivered with a laugh: "We are not Nigerian."

Accra is a dirty, chaotic city of about 2 million built on the shore of the Atlantic Ocean. As the business capital of Ghana, it has people in Western suits and dress robes. As the university capital of Ghana, it's full of students. And as the urban capital of Ghana, it has more than its share of begging, and peeing in the streets is so common that in the rare places where it is forbidden, spray-painted stenciled lettering demands DO NOT URINATE HERE. The streets are loud, bustling with vendors selling chocolate, fans, even kitchen-sink strainers. Billboards advertise deworming medicine.

We arrived at our hotel midmorning, threw our bags in the rooms, and decided to cool off from the equatorial heat with a swim in the kidney-shaped hotel pool, where a stone waterfall added an element of style. There were no other kids at the hotel, just a few African and European businessmen. So, Hannah and Joseph had to create their own fun, and Joseph declared a chicken fight in the pool. We all waded into about four feet of water and squared off in teams, Joan on my shoulders versus Hannah on Joseph's.

Then we switched and battled some more. We pushed, shoved, squealed, cheated, squealed even louder.

At lunch I decided we could use a reminder of why we were there. It can be easy to forget the big picture when you're knee-deep in action, as we would be the next day, when we headed to the villages to meet our new partners. I thought we needed a moment of reflection and context before the whirlwind. In my backpack I had squirreled away a couple of quotes that my friend Mark Albion had included in his inspiring newsletter, *Make a Life, Make a Living.*

As the kids were digging into the chocolate tarts they had found listed at the bottom of the menu, I pulled out two sheets and read aloud. First I quoted from Dr. Martin Luther King, Jr., explaining how he wanted to be remembered:

> Every now and then I think about my own death, and I think about my own funeral. And if you get somebody to deliver the eulogy, tell them not to talk too long. Tell them not to mention that I have a Nobel Peace Prize. Tell them not to mention that I have three or four hundred other awards. I'd like for somebody to say that day that Martin Luther King, Jr., tried to give his life serving others. I'd like for somebody to say that Martin Luther King, Jr., tried to love somebody . . . Say that I was a drum major for justice . . . for peace . . . for righteousness . . . I just want to leave a committed life behind.

"Ooh, I like that a lot," Hannah mumbled, her mouth full of tart.

"Good, good," Joseph added. "What's the next one?"

"You'll really like the next one, Joe. It's from J. K. Rowling," I said. I had selected this one intentionally for Joseph, given that he and I had read the entire Harry Potter series together aloud, under the comforter in Joan's and my bed —six years of important memories.

"Okay, here goes. She's talking at a school graduation, but I think it can apply to any of us."

The education you have earned and received gives you unique status and unique responsibilities . . . That is your privilege and your burden. If you choose to use your status and influence to raise your voice on behalf of those who have no voice; if you choose to identify not only with the powerful, but with the powerless; if you retain the ability to imagine yourself into the lives of those who do not have your advantages, then it will not only be your proud families who celebrate your existence, but thousands and millions of people whose reality you have helped transform for the better. We do not need magic to change the world; we carry all the power we need inside ourselves already: we have the power to imagine better.

"That one's even better than Martin's," Joseph said. "It really is our responsibility to do something for people who don't have as much as we have. But I have to say her 'do not need magic' thing is a little cheesy—you know, with her Harry Potter stuff."

"That's ridiculous, Joe," Hannah snapped. "Her point is that anyone can do this, that there's no magic to it. You know, like it's just what we all can do."

"I'm just saying I don't like her reference to magic," Joseph insisted.

"But her point is so much more than that, Joe. She's talking about people living in a bubble and not having a clue how others really live. Dad, read it again, will you?"

I did, and Hannah quoted after me as I said the line "'thousands and millions of people whose reality you have helped transform for the better.' See, that's my point, Joe. That's why we're here—we can't help millions, but we *can* do something good with a bunch of people to help them make their lives better."

Joseph recognized he was being a bit too literal about Rowling's use of the word *magic*, so he stayed silent. Joan, again referencing the quote, asked if we felt a burden in the privileges we had and how we might use them to help the powerless. The kids talked about our financial assets, their top-tier schools, their world of plenty.

For the next fifteen minutes or so we debated our role on the planet. Some of it was well-trod ground, some teasing banter. But it raised our spirits so much that Joan even agreed to let the kids share another chocolate tart to let the dialogue run.

That night we settled into our rooms and watched a few minutes of TV until Joan insisted that everyone write in their journal. She wanted first impressions as they had happened. Joseph explained how the hotel felt a bit like Disney's Animal Kingdom Lodge, where we had stayed in Orlando, and described some lizards with orange heads that he had seen. Hannah, as usual, focused more on people, writing of pushy jewelry vendors on the beach and a waiter with an easy smile who had taught her how to say *thank you* in the tribal language Twi: *medase*.

The next day would be a big one. We would leave at eight-thirty for the two-hour drive to the villages of the Eastern Region. It was there that we would learn the answer to our nagging question: what do we do?

HANNAH'S TAKE

Learning from an Extremist

ABOUT TWO YEARS AGO MY MOM SHOWED ME A STORY IN THE *New York Times Magazine* on Zell Kravinsky, a man with a remarkable view of the world: he sees everyone as equal, including himself.

Kravinsky earned tens of millions of dollars in the real estate business over the past several decades. But then he started giving it away. He made a large donation to help a school for special-needs children, created a $6.2 million endowment to support disease control and prevention, and donated a million square feet of real estate to Ohio State University's College of Public Health, at a value of $30 million. In all, Kravinsky gave away a majority of his net worth.

But he wasn't done. One day he read in the *Wall Street Journal* that 59,255 Americans were on the list for a kidney donation and that 3,641 had died while waiting in the past year. He became interested in the subject, and during his research Kravinsky found out that the risk of dying while donating a kidney is one in four thousand. That statistic outraged him; the idea of valuing one's own life at four thousand times that of someone else seemed wrong.

So he told his wife he was considering having one of his kidneys removed. His wife immediately objected, arguing that someday one of their own children might need a kidney and he might be the only possible donor. But Kravinsky looked at the four-thousand-to-one ratio again and went forward with the kidney donation.

The writer of the *Times* article asked Kravinsky a related question: would he allow his own child to die if it would enable one thousand other children to live? "Yes," he said. Not only that, but Kravinsky argued that he would allow his child to die if it permitted only two other children to live. The *Times* wrote, "What marks Kravinsky from the rest of us is that he takes the equal value of all human life as a guide to life, not just as a nice piece of rhetoric."

As I read the story, I became fascinated with this man. His self-sacrifice inspired me to become a blood donor, and I hope that one day I'll give a kidney as well. I felt a real connection with him, even though we had almost nothing in common. When I read the piece, Kravinsky was fifty-one and an unbelievably successful businessman; I was sixteen and still in high school. But we did have one thing in common: we wanted to help.

No one, I hope, expects any of us to be as selfless as Zell Kravinsky, but I think it's worth taking a minute to appreciate his view. It's extremely rare that you come across someone who thinks like this. Is he crazy or generous?

Activity

1. Journal your most honest answers to these questions: If there was a fire in your school or where you work, would you run out as fast as you could or would you stay back to save others? What evidence is there in your life so far to prove that you would do as you wrote? How many people would you take a bullet for? Where exactly are you on the "willingness to sacrifice for others" scale?

2. Think about the one person you love the most in your life. How many lives would you be willing to save in exchange for that one?

8

In the Villages

—— — — — — —— — — -

To have real adventure, there has to be some
uncertainty, some personal testing.

— **Max Miller**

THE NEXT MORNING we arrived at our first stop,
Kyeremase, by SUV. This wasn't the United States,
where we cocoon ourselves in sport utility vehicles for safety in car crashes or because we need plenty of
room for the kids, the dogs, and the traveling living rooms
we Americans love to cart with us. This was Ghana, where
the roads dole out such punishment that vehicle suspen-
sions can't handle the pounding without extra clearance.
And even SUVs couldn't keep any of us from feeling a bit
like a stuffed animal in a puppy's mouth.

We had certainly expected the villages to be remarkable,
but the drive itself was a fascinating cultural experience.
Each community we passed featured its own specialty,
depending on its agricultural output, with locals standing along the roads selling bottled palm oil (in Manso) or
bundles of charcoal (in Atakura). As we traversed the ru-

ral landscape, we encountered trucks piled high with more than a hundred used bicycles; those two-wheelers would be traded for cows in remote villages to help farmers get to their fields. We passed shabby trucks bearing the names of businesses in Korean, Dutch, and German, shipped to Ghana from those countries for a second life and giving the roads the feel of a vehicular Tower of Babel.

Taxis provided the most entertainment for us. Dilapidated Daewoos, they were painted with multicolored panels, a mess of browns, greens, yellows, and oranges. But like many businesses in Ghana, the taxis featured a short phrase stenciled onto the rear window proclaiming the driver's faith: *Psalm 23. Rejoice in the Lord. Lion of Judea.* And, my personal favorite, *Jesus I Grade You High.* I joked to Joan that we could get a decent Sunday school education just reading the cabs around the countryside. And maybe faith was crucial for the passengers for more than the usual reasons: despite the equatorial heat, the taxis were never air-conditioned, although they were usually packed to capacity plus one.

Headed for Kyeremase, we veered from the paved highway for a ninety-minute drive down what Ghanaians call a road but that felt more like a widened mountain-biking trail. The dirt generally was packed down, but the ruts were so deep from rains that our driver, Victor, was forced to maneuver the Nissan deftly around the worst of the gullies.

Every twenty minutes or so the road worsened, when we reached a town where paving had once been attempted but the concrete surface had deteriorated so badly that the ruts were even deeper than in the dirt sections. In these village areas, vendors would emerge with salt-dusted hard-boiled eggs or five-cent bags (yes, bags) of water. "I wanna learn that," Hannah said, watching women and boys carry massive loads hands-free on their heads.

The Hunger Project had created an itinerary for us, so that we could visit projects in various stages of completion over the organization's five-year process toward self-reliance. The first one, in Kyeremase, will go down in family history because of Joan's gaffe.

The villagers had been building the L-shaped epicenter for about four months, making the cinder blocks and then laying them in neat rows. Local men smoothed the concrete walls with trowels as we walked through the rooms of the half-finished building. Like every epicenter, this one had been wired for electricity, a reflection of optimism. The nearest grid was miles and miles away, but if power ever came, the people of these villages were ready.

There was no formal program at Kyeremase, so we listened as J.S., Janet, and Isaac, members of the Hunger Project's team, took us through the unfinished bank, meeting room, nurse's quarters, and food storage facility.

As we stepped back outside, a disheveled farmer walked directly over to Joan and Hannah. His gaunt face, with its sunken eyes and prominent cheekbones, reflected the pain of illness. His long-sleeved blue pullover was stained, and the fly of his green-and-white plaid pants was held together with a pin. He leaned forward to say something to Joan, but she couldn't understand. They tried again. Finally Isaac went over to help.

Joan relaxed a bit as she heard the man's simple request.

"He wants to know if you could take his picture," Isaac translated.

"Is it okay?" Joan asked, checking protocol with Isaac. Yes, he replied. So Joan snapped a photo of the farmer, Jacob Assan.

That went well, Joan thought, and she decided that this was her perfect chance to share. She reached into her bag and pulled out our family picture. "Do you want one of us?" she innocently asked the farmer. Yes, Jacob nodded eagerly, and Joan handed him a print.

Unfortunately, when you're the intriguing outsiders, no movement goes unnoticed. The dozens of people following us around the epicenter witnessed Joan's gift. Joseph summed up nicely in his journal what happened next: "Mom tried to give the farmer a picture of us when she basically got mugged for all one hundred of them." Indeed, once Joan had handed Jacob our photograph, everyone wanted one. They quickly swarmed around her, hands extended, jostling one another for position. Joan's eyes widened and her face tensed as she scrambled frantically to hand out the shots. But she couldn't handle the pace, so the crowd built up and the action got more intense. Finally, after distributing most of her stock like a Vegas blackjack dealer at a full table, Joan realized that her cause was lost. Her hair was pulling out from her ponytail holder, strands flying. With an exasperated gasp of "That's it, I'm all done, no more," she stuffed her few remaining pictures into her bag.

Joseph, J-Coon, and I, standing about a hundred yards away, had watched the scene unfold, ready to help if there was any danger but amazed that Joan was being mobbed like

Britney Spears among teenaged girls. Joseph and I laughed at the absurdity of it: our family photo had nearly caused a riot. "What are they going to do with those pictures?" Joseph asked with a chuckle. My mind conjured an image of our family photo being taped to a dirt wall or to handmade furniture in small thatched huts, a four-by-six-inch piece of art featuring a smiling, nicely dressed white family, curling and fading over the years.

But Joan and Hannah were far from amused. As they walked out of the crowd, they looked shell-shocked and embattled. Hannah's mind was exploding with doubt. *What the heck was all that?* she thought. *Is there something wrong with these people?* The moment had been so foreign, so irrational.

Ever the calm one, John just smiled gently as Joan and Hannah walked over briskly and deliberately. "Maybe we should pick a more intimate moment to hand out the rest of them," he suggested. With a sigh, Joan agreed.

Maybe John hadn't meant his suggestion to apply to more than just the photo moment, but his recommendation was a metaphor for how we needed to keep thinking about our work in Africa. Handing out goods indiscriminately could trigger an unexpected and sometimes unpleasant reaction. Crowds could form; resources could be squandered. We were learning, sometimes multiple times, a critical lesson: we needed to pick our aims and methods carefully, or else it was easy to go totally off course and accomplish almost nothing.

Our next stop that sunny, sweltering morning was far calmer but no less remarkable. As we arrived at Dome, some two hundred villagers had already gathered for the Hunger Project's cornerstone training session, called "Vision, Commitment, Action," or VCA for short.

When the Hunger Project first identifies clusters of villages to begin its economic development work, the organization's country director, Dr. Naana Agyemang-Mensah, told me during the drive, typically a chief arrives bearing a list. "Here are the things we need," the chief announces, pressing to be given those items. That's not surprising, really. That's the mentality that has long permeated a culture conditioned to ask for handouts and equally conditioned to get them. Old habits die hard.

The chiefs' requests don't fluster Dr. Naana, an intense woman with master's and Ph.D. degrees from Michigan State University. Sitting with Joan and me in the back seat of the Nissan SUV, she wore a tight-fitting African skirt and top with large yellow medallions printed on orange and green rectangles. As she adjusted her black-framed glasses, Dr. Naana explained that the chiefs need to learn the Hunger Project's paradigm-shifting methodology. "I tell the chiefs, 'Let me show you how the Hunger Project works and why we are different.'" Then, with her hallmark blend of meticulousness and stridency, she lays out the Hunger Project's strategy for changing hearts and minds.

Well before any structures can be built or any funds go into the bank, villagers start the empowerment process through workshops and the "Vision, Commitment, Action" training. They must begin to believe that they can be more successful if they take the reins themselves. They must create a management board made up of villagers—and, radically, that board must comprise at least 50 percent women. It's a startling demand of equality in these male-dominated cultures, but one that has such a strong impact that the Hunger Project refuses to yield on it. Despite long-held biases against them, women are the change agents for development.

With all that empowerment work and female equality on the table, some village chiefs walk away, prepared to accept the status quo or to look for a handout from another nonprofit organization. But Dr. Naana is not one to give up. Undaunted by the initial rejection, she adopts a more urgent tone. "This is for your future! You cannot live as you have been living. You *must* understand. Your government doesn't want to help you unless you show them that you are doing the work. You must show them how much you can achieve, *then* demand that they provide the services"—meaning literacy classes, water, electricity, and agricultural support.

By "your government," Dr. Naana is speaking of the local authorities, not politicians in Accra. For decades no one in the nation's capital has taken notice of villages that are many miles down unpaved roads. But local officials will. "You elect these people," she urges the chiefs and villagers, her face tensing and her right index finger pointing. "They work for you. *Make them provide those things they are elected to provide.*"

As Dr. Naana described the way she prods her fellow Ghanaians, I realized that she was describing the second mentality shift. The first one was helping people believe they have the power to create their own path to success. But, of equal importance, Dr. Naana was pressing villagers to recognize that the government works for them. We take that concept for granted in the United States, but for centuries citizens in Ghana and other African countries have been cowed by their leaders, afraid to demand that their government officials serve them. What Dr. Naana is urging is a life-changer.

As we rode farther into the verdant Ghanaian countryside, Dr. Naana circled back to the example of the chief with his list of demands. I could feel the deep pride in her voice as she described returning to the villages six months after the chief had sought his initial handout. "We go back into those villages, and this time the chief hands us a list of things they have *accomplished*. 'Look what we have done.' They are proud of their own activities. Oh, this is good. We are making progress."

Now Dr. Naana was beaming, her head nodding rapidly. She was speaking of changing hearts and minds and futures. I realized how much tougher that kind of transformation is than digging a well and moving on to the next community. For the villagers, real change requires teamwork, shared sacrifice, and faith in one another. For the nonprofit groups, these efforts take time, consistency, reinforcement, patience. This is not aid; it is metamorphosis.

As Dr. Naana spoke, I realized with a jolt that she could have been describing our family, not African villagers. Our project had much the same trajectory and needs: teamwork, shared sacrifice, faith in one another. My mind returned to

HANNAH'S TAKE

Helping Kids Get Truly Empowered

MY PARENTS MADE A DECISION THAT WE WOULD SHARE POWER completely for this "Half" project. As Mark Twain said, "The most interesting information comes from children, for they tell all they know and then stop." Joseph and I had way more say than usual in what went on with the project, and we had a sense of leadership to go along with it. I instantly felt more responsible and mature; people actually cared what I had to say.

Once Joseph and I had more voice in family activities, it began directly enhancing other parts in our lives. It helped Joseph become a leader within his group of friends by starting a band and organizing practices. For me, it was more about how I felt in school. After we started our project, I ran for and got elected to the student government as one of my grade's representatives. Because of this project, I became more confident speaking my mind and felt more like a leader in my community.

Money and power go hand in hand. Those who have one frequently have the other. But most kids don't really understand money, and this is a good place to start the education. In our family, as in a lot of families, I think, we had to put aside one third of our allowance for charity. When kids donate to charity (in our family, we use the Hebrew word *tzedakah*), they can make choices they might not make if they are volunteering their time. It expands the number of organizations kids can connect to, since many groups won't allow people younger than sixteen to work. As I mentioned before,

Joseph and I have often used our money to buy groceries for the local food bank.

In addition to allowance, this could be a good opportunity for young people to build their business skills and get creative. For instance, kids who care about a local children's theater might not be able to volunteer there but could put on a talent show to raise money. They could "hire" their parents as roadies, pull in friends to help perform or market, and ask local businesses to sponsor the fundraiser.

When kids have say over where their money goes, they can truly feel that it is their decision that is making the gifts happen.

Activity

Parents, for a birthday or religious holiday, give your kids a check with the amount filled out but the "pay to the order of" line left blank. Let them choose an organization or cause to receive the donation. As they are choosing where to give, let them discuss why that organization appeals to them. (By the way, it's probably a good idea to give your kids another gift too; otherwise they might see this process as punishment. This is especially true with younger children.)

that night at the dinner table when Joan urged me to share power with the kids. The parallels were stunning. Could the secrets to success be that universal?

Hannah, Joseph, Joan, and I took seats in white resin chairs at Dome; we were the guests of honor at a training event, sitting in the front row alongside a dozen or so chiefs and elders in ceremonial dress, one wearing a gorgeous chocolate-brown crownlike hat with moons and stars sewn on it. The rest of the audience stood or sat in a horseshoe facing us. Like it or not, we would be the center of attention again.

After a brief Christian prayer delivered in Twi (the closing prayer would be a Muslim one, reflecting the harmony between the religions here), Dr. Naana was on her feet, barking into the wireless microphone. She is not a subtle woman and, as with the chiefs, at this meeting she pressed the villagers to do their share, to work their assigned days building the epicenter buildings. "Serve yourself with all your energy," she demanded, pointing her finger around the crowd. "If you serve yourself, it is not slavery, it is self-reliance. If you are lazy and wait for someone to feed you, what happens on the day they don't come to feed you?"

It must have been ninety-five degrees under the broad red-and-blue-striped tent, which had been erected directly in front of the unfinished epicenter building. Since we were unable to understand the Twi being spoken during the meeting, our minds wandered. Joseph, fanning himself with his black journal, began to recognize that there would be little opportunity for kickball or reading with kids.

In fact, the answer to the "What do we do?" question was coming into focus, although in a mushy and vague way: support. I know that may seem like nothing—and to us for a while it did—but we weren't there to provide emergency relief, to clean up after a hurricane or help rebuild tsunami-crushed homes. We had chosen to help alleviate rural poverty and hunger, and we had to keep reminding ourselves that the answer lay in a combination of financial support and hands-off backing. To put it in financial terms, it felt a bit like smart venture capital: research where to invest, provide the cash, and then let the experienced management team run the show. To do something more would be to get in the way or, worse, to actually bolster dependence.

I'd be lying if I didn't admit that for all of us, especially the kids, there was a twinge of disappointment as we learned our role. It's harder to see yourself as a change agent when you're not actually in the lead. Building a wall is fun; digging a well feels productive. We needed to keep reminding ourselves of the failures of the "Africans ask, Westerners do" mindset. This was change from the neck up.

A few minutes into the program, Dr. Naana leaned over and asked if I would speak. Sure, I said. Then it hit me: I had no idea what to say. I spent much of the next forty-five minutes thinking about what to tell these hundreds of people whose lives I had dropped into like a space traveler. We had nothing in common, no shared experience. Their reference points and mine were an ocean apart. But my overriding emotion was worry, not about public speaking but about my role in this play. Should I be tough and exhortative, like

Dr. Naana? That didn't feel right. I knew I shouldn't be Mr. Handout or Mr. Condescending, but what Mr. should I be?

I hadn't resolved all of these crosscurrents when my turn came and the wireless mike was passed to me. I scanned the crowd. Many of the villagers' T-shirts clearly had come from the United States: *Xavier Basketball; 1996 Fairless Hills, Pa., All-Star Champs,* with an air-brushed baseball carica-ture; *No Jesus, No Life;* and a bright pink shirt announcing *Always Maxi Pads* in front and *Get 2 for Free* on the back.

As I collected my thoughts, I considered my conversa-tion with Dr. Naana on the car ride, her descriptions of the meetings with chiefs. Suddenly John Coonrod's explana-tions of our family's role became clear to me: "You are their guest. If your chair breaks, just stay where you are until someone brings you another one. That's what a host would do for you," he had told us. "Remember, you are not here to do things for them. That's what they are accustomed to. It has to be the other way around for real change to happen."

Standing there with the mike in my hand, I got it. To offer these villagers anything but support at this point would have undermined the Hunger Project's repeated messages of self-sufficiency. So, I kept my remarks brief, lauding the villagers for their achievements so far, urging them to keep working, and reminding them that we would be watching their progress. No one will ever confuse my speech at Dome with the Gettysburg Address, but I was one sweaty, relieved fellow.

I hadn't sat down for more than a minute when the next shock came. "When the speeches and prayers are over, there will be dancing," Isaac said, leaning forward between Joan and me from the row behind us. "And because you are the guests, you will need to start the dancing."

Whoa. Start the dancing? I had visions of Joan and my wedding at the Cedar Rapids, Iowa, country club twenty-one years earlier, that oh-so-awkward, oh-so-public first dance, our four feet moving in almost random directions. I think we had danced five times since then. At other people's weddings, I'm the guy who stands on the outside of the circle, clapping and praying that no one will try to rope me in. The only good thing is that Joan is standing there with me, equally satisfied with being on the perimeter of the dance floor. Of all the worries I had harbored about bringing our family to Africa, dancing self-consciously as the center of attention had never occurred to me.

In a mix of shock and fear, I blurted out, "Um, Isaac, have you noticed? I'm white."

Isaac laughed heartily, then put his hand lightly on my shoulder. "Kevin, in Ghana, we have an expression you might like: 'Everything you do that is not walking is dancing.'"

That was the kind of low bar that my musically challenged feet needed to hear. But I noticed that I was sweating slightly harder in my navy blue Land's End polo shirt.

In a few minutes the speeches were over and music began to blare from the stacked speakers. J-Coon stood and we took his cue, following him into an open field. As I walked, I realized that our first-dance song was Christian praise music—not exactly the genre I would have picked. It's hard enough for me to dance, let alone shimmy to praise music.

Hannah felt no stress about this, bouncing out into the field. She was in her comfort zone, jumping into an activity she knew well. At least it was better than listening to speeches in a foreign language. Hannah and Dr. Naana's daughter, also named Naana, bopped onto the grassy dance floor, where they were joined by a woman wearing a traditional West African head wrap.

But Joan, Joseph, and I walked far more tentatively to the center of the field. Despite Isaac's reassurance about the low expectations, we couldn't have felt more awkward. For a few critical seconds, roles had reversed: now *we* were the ones in need of support; we were the vulnerable ones—not in a life-or-death way, of course, but uncomfortable nonetheless.

Within a few seconds several villagers must have sensed that, and help appeared. A woman in curlers came out of the crowd to dance opposite Joan; next to her, a woman carrying a tray of juice boxes on her head twirled by herself. Next came Joseph's partner: a man in his twenties wearing a black polo shirt and jeans.

I hadn't gotten far into the field when a woman with a low V-cut blouse slipped in front of me and began to dance. Her smile was engaging, and she even flicked her eyebrows at me a couple of times. Was this flirting or dancing? (Joan later dubbed her my "Ghanaian wife.") When the first song ended, my dance partner/savior came up beside me, put her arm around my shoulder, and flicked her eyebrows a few more times. I smiled back in a combination of relief and connection.

If our self-conscious dancing was not really adequate, at

least villagers said it to one another in Twi. We never heard anything.

By the time we left Dome for lunch on that first day, Joseph had become an insider in one important way: he had picked up on the three-step Ghanaian handshake. The grip starts with a traditional businessman's grip and transitions to a soul shake, with interlocking thumbs. Then the fun happens: as the men pull away, they create an audible snap off the other person's index and middle fingers. As we shook hands, Joseph would pop his way through the crowd, much to the delight of the men, who often smiled broadly and exclaimed, "Ah, you know our handshake already! Very good, very good."

Later we learned that we had a role beyond being supportive speakers and dancers. We were muscle. Not roll-up-your-sleeves, carry-bricks muscle. But Mafia-style, look-who-I-have-in-my-corner muscle.

As we drove up to the Non-Formal Functional Literacy Programme office, I could tell we were approaching a small-scale seat of power. Oh sure, there were the usual goats and hens in the yard. But there, propped in the window, was an air conditioner, keeping the local political appointees comfortable inside. Our family hadn't been told much about this meeting, which was listed on the day's schedule as "Courtesy Call on one of THP's key partners."

The office of the district commissioner in charge of adult literacy was painted teal, yet it remained drab. After brief introductions, the two officials sat behind a large, cluttered wooden desk, facing us. For nearly an hour they and Dr. Naana spoke in English about programming and resources.

At first I listened hard for anything interesting. I learned at one point that the Hunger Project had trained 120 reading facilitators and served more than 3,000 learners. Dr. Naana described a thirty-seven-year-old villager who had never attended school but received two years of adult literacy training, then went to secondary school and was now embarking on a career of computer programming.

But most of the conversation went over our heads. Joseph and Hannah had a hard time disguising their boredom this time, staring with glassy eyes at the posters on the wall (ELECTION 2008, VOTE PEACEFULLY, said one adorned with pictures of a dove and a hand placing a ballot in a box). They sighed; they fidgeted. Joseph disconnected so thoroughly that he didn't realize the discussion focused on education; he wrote in his journal that night that the meeting had concerned new roads.

When we finally shook hands with the officials and left the building, Hannah was bursting with relief. "Holy crap, dude, that was sooooo boring."

But Joan was grinning. "Oh no, that was so good. We were props—you know, tools."

"What?" Hannah asked, wondering what Joan had seen.

"Dr. Naana knows exactly what she's doing. She needed us to be there to show those politicians who her teammates were. We were the Americans on her team. That's her way of pushing for more resources. So good."

Service, it occurred to me, was a strange creature. Our trip to that government office might have been the most important stop on our Ghanaian tour. As boring as it had been for us, it was vital for Dr. Naana to show who the Hunger Project had on its side. She would parlay our family's attendance into more literacy experts, more educated villagers—not by *our* doing any reading (as we had expected earlier) but by having locals teach locals. That would be change that could have long-lasting results on several levels.

If the hardship we endured was an hour of boredom in a rural politician's office, so be it. If the only muscles that ached at the end of this trip were in our butts, fine. Sitting in meetings certainly wasn't what we'd had in mind when we started our journey of service, but we now knew how meaningful that could be.

For the next several days we stayed at the Modak Royal Hotel, a string of one-story bungalows in the hills of the Eastern Region. At John's urging, we agreed not to spend nights in the villages, since he worried that that would be disruptive to the work and life there. We were the first Americans many of the villagers had met; if we stayed in those hut-filled clusters, unavoidably we would be seen as honored guests, visitors needing the best the community could offer. Tempting as it was, it would be unconscionable to drop that kind of burden onto the people we were encouraging—to eat their hard-won food, to accept gifts they would no doubt offer. (Truth be told, staying in a village environment with no water, lights, or flush toilets might have proved too primitive anyway for our soft Western family, which had never even gone camping.)

Still, it was disappointing to miss what happened when the sun went down in these isolated locales, to sidestep the chance to relate better to the villagers' daily lives. As we retreated to the Modak, there was a stark recognition that it would take a long time to be anything other than foreigners standing outside the villages' bubble, our noses pressed to the glass. Maybe we could bridge the gap on a future trip, but for now we grudgingly accepted that splitting up for the evenings was for the best.

That was a fairly natural result of the choices we had made. After all, we hadn't committed to leaving the United States to live in Ghana to work with these communities for an extended period. We had reached a boundary that hadn't been part of our planning or conversation but had now clearly emerged: we would be outside supporters, or investors, as the Hunger Project calls them.

John, Dr. Naana, and the rest of the Hunger Project team always knew that, of course. That was the way they had structured the organization from the beginning. Ghanaians do the work in Ghana. Malawians do the work in Malawi. Period, end of story. Local people create change and in turn reap the benefits or consequences of their actions. The rest, including our family (and even John, really), would always be no more than members of the supporting cast. Brian Cashman is the general manager of the New York Yankees, but he never swings a bat or throws a pitch.

As we settled into our role as observers and supporters, we began to develop an even stronger sense of how we could best help. It's fascinating in hindsight to see the shifts in how we understood our function over the year of planning. At the beginning, we saw ourselves as doers, ready to roll up our sleeves and work; as we learned more, we were ready to be kickball-playing friends; now we realized that the best role we could play was as financially supportive fans, cheering the contributions of the players. And sometimes as a prop for people who needed us.

Writing checks and cheering? Wasn't that where we had started nearly two years earlier, after Hannah encountered the homeless man and the Mercedes? Hannah had scoffed when we told her about the money we donated each year to Habitat and others. We needed to be a family that *did* the hard work, she demanded.

Now it was startling to recognize that the method was at least partly right after all. Willing hands certainly have a place when the organizational structure is correct, as at a Habitat build alongside the homeowner. But projects must be carefully crafted, assuring that empowerment is front and center even when outsiders are involved. Generosity can't be a simple paint-by-numbers exercise. The solutions are too nuanced for that. And in some cases, as in working in developing nations with chronic poverty, writing checks to fund grass-roots development and offering simple moral support might just be the best way to help people improve their own futures. Who knew?

Hannah had another revelation the very next day. During our tour around rural Ghana, we stopped to watch a skit performed by Hunger Project–trained villagers. It was a simple play in which a father refuses to pay his daughter's school fees because he believes that it is more important to educate his sons. The girl, desperate for opportunity, becomes a prostitute and contracts HIV. The skit was designed, of course, to teach the importance of gender equality and encourage parents to see their daughters the same way they see their sons.

Despite the earnestness of the message, the performance was filled with larger-than-life actors; both the exaggerated pimp and the pillow-stuffed pregnant girl played their parts for comedy. Even though we didn't understand Twi, the humor was physical, and we laughed often as the amateur actors moved around on the patch of dirt that served as their stage.

Hannah, though, spent a chunk of her time watching the audience as well as the performers. "They were laughing just like I was laughing," she told me later, describing the sense of connection and the bond she felt. "I know it's incredibly obvious, but I realized that these people had the same sense of humor that I had."

There, in rural Ghana, Hannah was reliving the kind of simple interaction she had experienced years earlier at Café 458, on that afternoon when she had heard the homeless men discussing the basketball game she and I had watched the night before. People are people, Hannah saw again. Even this far from home. Even with virtually no possessions. Now she could set aside the shock of that irrational photo-distribution scene. These villagers in Ghana "were just like me. Different circumstances, different opportunity, but just like me."

We spent days in the villages, evenings at the Modak. The breakfasts of fried eggs, dry toast, and room-temperature baked beans at the hotel restaurant were surprisingly edible. We are by no means the most adventurous food family, but as the days passed we grew comfortable sampling fufu, a porridgelike staple made from cassava and yam, and ken-key, a corn-based dumpling, from the bowls of one of our Hunger Project friends. Well, not Hannah, but the rest of us sampled those. We all decided, though, to pass on grasscut-ter, a rodentlike animal usually sold on the side of the road, splayed out on sticks.

In the evenings Hannah and Joseph popped on the small TVs bolted into the corner of the rooms and laughed heart-ily as they watched a Ghanaian soap opera on one of the five available channels (two of which were the same). The first night Joseph took a cold shower; hours later we figured out how to turn on the water heater, with a switch outside the room.

There were, of course, minor discomforts. For one, we were becoming increasingly thin-skinned—literally. The malaria-prevention medication was reducing our ability to withstand punctures. Small scratches that our faces or arms might have easily tolerated before caused bright-red stripes on our pale skins. But we experienced far fewer health problems than we had expected. No severe stomach dis-comfort, no death-threatening bug bite. Our traveling med-icine chest remained virtually untouched.

The second night at the Modak, John reviewed with us the itinerary for the next day. On the agenda: Hannah would speak at the dedication of a new school.

An hour later Joan and Joseph were lying on the pink hotel sheets and Hannah was poised at a small desk. She folded a sheet of paper lengthwise and began to write out notes for her talk. She wrote, edited, and rehearsed until midnight, then again over breakfast as she sipped Nestlé

Milo, a beverage that resembles hot chocolate. A half-dozen practice rounds later, she was ready.

To picture the new primary school in Aweregya, you might think about your own elementary school experience. Picture the teacher, the other students, the classrooms, the building. Now strip out the air-conditioning, lights, operative windows, PA system, cafeteria, running water, and electricity. In fact, just forget about almost everything except the blackboards, desks, and schoolyard (although the one in Aweregya is a grass field with no play equipment). That's the new primary school at Aweregya.

Still, it's a marvelous building that has moved this community way beyond any of its neighbors for miles and miles. It has taken five years to build this facility, which cost 52,000 Ghanaian cedi (about $52,000). The process underwent plenty of stops and starts.

When Aweregya's residents first asked Hunger Project officials to help fund the project, they were told that a three-room schoolhouse would work just fine. But local leaders pushed back. "We need six rooms," they said. "Fine," replied Dr. Naana. "Raise more money." So the villagers did, somewhat to the surprise of Dr. Naana and her team. They laid the cinder-block walls, built the window openings, constructed the partially transparent ceiling, and attached the biggest blackboards we'd ever seen. In the end, the Hunger Project paid about 70 percent of the cost, the rest being covered by funds from villagers and a small federal grant.

As we gathered for the dedication, we could tell this was an important event. More than twenty tribal chiefs and elders had come and were sitting in the front row, facing the school. They were by far the most formally dressed of the four-hundred-plus attendees, proudly sporting full-length ceremonial clothes, which were draped, as always, toga-style over the left shoulder. As we got out of the cars, a hundred schoolchildren in peach-colored jumpers stared. We were accustomed to the gaping by now, the pointing of the kids, the squeals of *obruni* (white person) as the young people gawked at our pale skin.

We entered the ceremony at the end of a line that was greeting the chiefs. Behind us, a makeshift ten-member marching band played with deafening drum and horn cacophony. These teenagers in black pants and purple T-shirts clearly lived by the motto of "loud and proud," particularly the guy with cymbals, one of which was marred by a three-inch chunk that had been removed.

Greeting the chiefs was a bit like going through a wedding receiving line, without the small talk, introductions, or even exchange of names. These moments were for physical connection and a nonverbal acknowledgment of authority and respect. Many of the chiefs looked warmly into our eyes, some with a smile or a nod. Others never made eye contact, and we were left wondering if they were aloof, shy, or disdainful. What did they think of us? I wished I could ask whether they saw us as true partners or just the latest set of Western deep pockets or a lottery ticket that let them help their people. We knew how we *wanted* them to view us, but we never got to ask what they truly believed. That was a shame.

Regardless, we headed for our seats, the only wooden chairs at the event—dining room chairs, actually. Behind us, villagers stood four or five deep, including a man wearing a Superman T-shirt. "Check it out, Han, Superman lives in this village. Who knew?" I quipped in an attempt to relax the fifteen-year-old. I figured she was jittery. She ignored me.

Shortly after we settled in, the true guest of honor arrived—the regional chief. The head of 278 villages, the *Oboo hene* entered with his own procession, and what a sight it was. In stark contrast to this dirt-poor community, the *Oboo hene* wore a beautifully patterned Akan kente cloth, the rich rose, indigo, and earthy green pattern bursting from the fabric. His left hand sported a gold sunburst ring so oversized that it covered part of two adjacent fingers. His three-man entourage included the interlocutor, the *Oboo hene*'s top aide and occasional mouthpiece, clutching in his left hand a six-foot-tall gold staff topped by a carving of one child boosting another up a tree limb.

I glanced at my watch as we all sat down for the start of the event. As usual, we were running about an hour late. But that wasn't surprising, given that for the past three days we had been on perpetually tardy West Africa time, a measure that leaves a level of flexibility that U.S. airlines would love to have for their on-time-arrival data.

Hannah and the rest of us waited in the front row, facing the audience, conspicuous as usual because of our foreignness. Even during dull stretches in the program, we found ourselves forced to appear attentive, playing to any crowd that might be watching. It was an awkward feeling, always being in someone's view. Several times I subtly knocked my knee into Joseph's leg when he openly yawned or absent-mindedly flipped around the viewfinder of his video camera.

As the speeches rolled on, they weren't without their moments of entertainment. At one point the local member of Parliament called the Hunger Project "Christlike" and proceeded to butcher a New Testament story. But he spoke in English, so many in the crowd probably didn't notice. Switching to Twi, he proceeded to take credit for the school, triggering mumbled annoyance from Dr. Naana, who knew where the funds and effort had come from.

When the *Oboo hene* spoke, he chose not to use his interlocutor. Instead he spoke smoothly into the blue-foam-topped mike, his Oxford-trained English crisp and dignified. "Today is one of my happiest days in this community," he orated. "I cast my eyes on this school when I arrived. There are two hundred and seventy-eight towns and communities in Oboo, not one with a school as nice as this one." He concluded with a line that brought hope—and reminded us why we had come: "When we leave here, I am going to ensure that we put up classroom buildings that will beat this one." Not much more than words, to be sure, but ones we could hang hope on.

At last we had come to line nine in the program: "Address by the THP Investors." This description struck me as a bit odd. We hadn't invested in this school project at all. Nor had we invested in Abisu, where Hannah had cut the ribbon at the corn mill, or in Dome, where I had urged the villagers to keep up their work and push toward self-reliance. Not a penny of Salwen money had gone into Aweregya. Our villages would be determined later.

Yet we were honored guests, and we figured we might as well use the opportunity to demonstrate to these communities that people six thousand miles away give a damn about them. In Aweregya, the politicos were snaring some credit, but clearly this community hadn't been anybody's focus for long.

The emcee for the event, Osei Bonsu, offered a brief introduction of Hannah in Twi, and she leapt out of her chair to take her place by his side. At least we thought it was an introduction of Hannah, because a) we were at the right place in the program, and b) he said her name. We had no idea what he said before or after her name.

Hannah wore a fuchsia top and cream-colored slacks; her hair was untied and hanging around her shoulders. She held her speech in her left hand and had a teal rubber "Make a Difference" bracelet around her wrist. Public speaking is nerve-racking for almost everyone—it routinely tops the list of phobias—and the size of this audience couldn't have been alleviating the tension. Even the old Toastmasters rule "Know your audience" had been thrown out the window; we had never met these people before.

Yet Hannah appeared poised as she dispensed the thank-yous and the greetings from the United States and from our family. "I would first like to speak to the adults, and then the children," she told the audience. "To the adults: I know how important education is. Education means opportunity. With this primary school, you have created more opportunity for your children. I am impressed with the success you have reached. We support your work and will be watching you as you move forward."

Now Hannah was rolling, looking up from her notes more often, slowing down. And then she whirled, turning away from the adults to where the schoolkids were watching near the new building. She looked directly at them and began anew. "And to the children: First, read every book you can find. Second, listen to your teachers. Third, never forget you can succeed." Then, quickly glancing back at the chiefs, she closed with a hasty "Thank you again."

As Hannah headed back to her seat, Joan gave her a big thumbs-up. A year earlier Joan had spearheaded the effort to empower our daughter, a move aimed at teaching our kids leadership. Hannah and Joseph were earning the authority to use their voices in important matters.

Here in Aweregya, Hannah had chosen to use her voice to empower others. In a spirit of partnership, she had encouraged adults to keep their eye on the next generation as they strengthened their future. She had prodded kids to strive for better. Now that she recognized her power, she was choosing to use it to bolster others. I could see pride filling Joan's face.

The program continued with a dance, a drumming show, and a Christian prayer in Twi, but we were hardly listening anymore. Hannah was relieved to have her public pronouncements behind her. Joseph was thrilled that the event was almost over, so he could be out of the spotlight. Joan and I joined the *Oboo hene* in cutting the ribbon to commission the school. Dozens of people streamed into the new schoolrooms, and the celebration was under way, the band back in business, pounding and blowing with deafening volume again.

Fifteen minutes later we headed for the SUVs, ready to leave the people of Aweregya to revel in their achievement. As usual, dozens of kids gathered around us, posing for Hannah's Nikon and shaking hands with Joseph, the tall teenager with the braces in the Under Armour shirt.

But as we waited near the cars for our group to collect, an unusual thing happened. A few kids who looked to be about seven years old got very close to us and put out their hands, palms up. In English, one of them demanded: "Give me a cedi."

"Are you asking me for money?" I replied, straining to hear what he had said.

"Yes, give me a cedi," the boy repeated.

I flashed back to the homeless man on the Buford Highway Connector holding his sign: HUNGRY, HOMELESS, PLEASE HELP. With his hand-lettered request, he had unknowingly started our family on this journey. Now, thousands of miles from both home and him, we were confronted with a similar request. This time there was no steering wheel to grip, no McDonald's Arch cards to give away. But we had nearly two years of education behind us, having learned from veterans like Joan Holmes and John Coonrod, understanding the causes of hunger and poverty, recognizing the solutions. Handing over a dollar or a cedi wasn't the right answer.

"No," I said firmly, more startled than annoyed.

Inside the car, when she heard the story, Dr. Naana fumed. "Begging!" she exclaimed, seething. "That is so embarrassing. Begging!" Under her breath, she mumbled the word several times as she stared out the window.

Her face remained tense, and I wondered what was going through her mind. Was she thinking that the Hunger Project was falling short in its efforts to teach self-reliance in Aweregya? Was she thinking that it was a rogue kid who hadn't gotten the lessons despite her repeated urging? Or was she just thinking that there was a hell of a lot of work to do?

She'd be right about the last one.

HANNAH'S TAKE

Inspiring Others to Join You

THERE ARE 6 BILLION PEOPLE IN THIS WORLD, AND YOU ARE ONE person. It's easy to think, "How much of a difference can I *really* make?" The short answer is, a lot. I love the quote from Marian Wright Edelman, the children's rights advocate: "We must not, in trying to think about how we can make a big difference, ignore the small daily differences we can make which, over time, add up to big differences that we often cannot foresee."

Kristin Walter, or Kristin Grilled Cheese as my family calls her, is the director of a cool nonprofit group called FeelGood. On college campuses, students working with FeelGood sell grilled cheese sandwiches to raise money for hunger-related causes. Along with her cofounder, Talis Apud-Martinez, Kristin started small, opening a chapter at the University of Texas, and the group has now expanded to twenty-one colleges. Kristin has figured out how to inspire others to buy into the FeelGood vision with the motto "Ending world hunger one grilled cheese at a time."

Kristin explains that grilled cheese is a "comforting food," while hunger is a heavy topic. While the sandwich is on the griddle, the volunteers talk to the customers about their philosophy of ending hunger by empowering people in poverty. (You can learn more at www.feelgoodworld.org.)

We talked to Kristin about how she started and why selling a few grilled cheese sandwiches ever felt like something that could end world hunger. Before opening FeelGood, she said, she had often asked herself whether she should be doing more. She says that she realized that ending hunger isn't just about feeding the hundreds of millions of people who are hungry, but about empowering them to realize their potential as change makers. That fits with our family philosophy, by the way: it's not about handing food to hungry people, but instead about inspiring them to get themselves out of poverty.

Like Kristin, I don't ever feel like I'm doing enough to solve the world's poverty problems. Although I know there is always more that can be done, I'm proud of the work I'm doing as an individual. Think about the work that you're doing and compare it to your potential. Are you doing the right amount of work? As my dad always tells me, "All you can do is all you can do."

9

Transformation Observed

— — — · — — — ·

Strange is our situation here upon earth. Each of us
comes for a short visit, not knowing why, yet sometimes
seeming to divine a purpose. From the standpoint of
daily life, however, there is one thing we do know — that
man is here for the sake of other men.

— Albert Einstein

O N THE FIFTH DAY in Africa, we said goodbye to
John Coonrod and the rest of the Hunger Project team and set off on our own. "When you get
home, say hello to Kanye for me," Joseph joked as he shook
John's hand. John didn't miss a beat: "Word to your mother,"
he deadpanned through his white beard.

We had decided to stay in Ghana, to learn about the
country and spend some money there, so we hired a driver
for a weeklong jaunt to discover the people and the culture.
We bounced across the exhilarating but stomach-churning
canopy bridges at Kakum National Park, perched in tree-
tops forty meters above the ground. We tasted the foul
stench of slavery at Assin Manso, where for three centu-

ries men and women had their last bath in the river just before being sold. We mourned at Elmina Castle, where those slaves were held in bondage before being shipped to the New World. But we also visited the amazing crafts villages of the Ashanti region, where we learned the meanings of patterns of kente cloth and Adinkra stamping.

Oh, and we got in a car accident. Forty-five minutes into our first day without Hunger Project supervision, our guide, Ben, was driving us north from Accra. As we passed through the town of Nsawam, an oncoming truck loaded with palm branches inexplicably pulled around a car and into our lane. Ben deftly swerved our Nissan Patrol, turning a head-on collision into a noisy but harmless sideswipe with no injuries. After a quick check on our well-being, Ben was livid, thinking about his two-week-old vehicle.

As people do in many warm-weather climates, Ghanaians spend most of their time outdoors. Homes are primarily for sleeping. So when the shop owners and residents of Nsawam heard the crash, they flocked to the scene, debating, pointing, reconstructing the incident. Ben and I got out of the Nissan and wandered back about fifty yards to see the ramshackle truck and look for the driver. But he had disappeared in the melee.

After a minute or so I glanced back at our SUV. There, in the middle of dozens of Ghanaian men, was Joseph, snapping handshakes. Hannah was nearby, talking with other men, chatting effusively and refusing their requests for her e-mail address. She had a huge grin on her face as she described the accident, which she later wrote was her "fave part of the trip so far." For all of us, the moment had been harrowing, a nearly serious wreck in a country with medical standards we weren't eager to test.

Looking back at Hannah and Joseph, though, I realized that they were growing, comfortable in an environment that might have paralyzed them earlier. After all, this was the same Hannah who had refused to visit friends if they had dogs. Now, out there on the streets of an impoverished country, our kids were embracing the foreign.

Several hours later we were back on the road, this time with a new driver, Justin, a soft-spoken man with a gentle smile. Like most Ghanaians, Justin, a professional driver, couldn't afford a car; when the tour company hired him, he took the *tro-tro* (bus) to his job, used the company's car, and headed back home on the *tro-tro*.

I sat in the passenger seat, and Joan took turns scratching the kids' backs, timing each for exactly eleven minutes according to the dashboard clock, taking a sixty-second rest, and then switching to the next kid's back for eleven more minutes. When Joan sat up front, Hannah and I shared iPod headphones, one earbud for her, one for me. I learned that Hannah almost never listens to a full song before jumping to the next one. Two verses, a chorus, and *boom,* she was gone. It crossed my mind that the five-year plan of the Hunger Project could be great for increasing her patience.

As we drove along the rural roads, I found beauty in the thatched-hut villages that sprang up every few miles. I tried to photograph them from the moving car, remarking on the well-kept symmetry of the mud walls and the palm-branch roofs. But Hannah and Joseph could see little of the picturesque villages that I enjoyed. Instead they saw the poverty, the poorly dressed children sitting on the ground staring at us as we drove by.

On a Thursday evening in Ghana's second largest city, Kumasi, we finally found an Internet signal. At long last we had a chance to stream the *Today* show and CNN pieces about our family project on our MacBooks, three days after the segments had aired.

Joseph and Hannah lay together on one bed at the Miklin Hotel, a frayed green comforter beneath them. Joan and I sat perched on another mattress in the adjacent room, the doors between the rooms propped open. We synchronized our mouse clicks so we could watch the clips at the same time, looking again for shared experience.

The news pieces themselves were great. On CNN, Rusty Dornin told our story crisply, mixing in shots of each family member and both houses. We appreciated that she showed the FOR SALE sign at Peachtree Circle with Sally's phone number on it; maybe it would help move the merchandise. But we cringed at how the editors had injected a tacky spinning "$800,000" into the narrative section to dramatize the amount we were giving away.

On NBC, John Larson and Amy Unell focused on Hannah, her demand for more action from our family, and her history of volunteerism, illustrated with short clips of her unscheduled "work" at the food bank and Café 458. Delightfully, the piece closed with a mention that Joseph had won the two-thousand-dollar grand prize from Coldwell Banker, with John's voiceover raising the specter of a total do-gooder family: "And what did Joseph do with the money?" Pause. "Nah, he bought a guitar." The video cut back to the studio, where Matt Lauer, Ann Curry, and Meredith Vieira were all sitting on the couch. They each offered a closing comment, with Curry having the last word. Pumping her fists toward the camera, she actually addressed our daughter: "Hannah, you rock!"

From the bed in Kumasi, Joseph quickly mimicked the line, eager to tease his sister. "Hannah, you rock," he shouted in a girly voice, punching his fists in the air even more exuberantly than Curry had. Then we laughed over how Larson had cleverly misdirected viewers into thinking that Joseph had given away his prize money before revealing the truth. As Matt Lauer had said from the couch, "I was beginning to think they were too perfect."

But the feel-good glow dissipated when we got to the hundreds of comments that viewers had posted online since the pieces had aired. We alternated reading them aloud. At first it seemed that most of the writers offered compliments or praised Hannah's caring. But soon our eyes felt magnetically drawn to the negative reactions. What is it about criticism that we hear so much more loudly than praise?

Many viewers took us to task for working in Africa, at first in muted critiques. Someone using the online name "dangelgregz" suggested that we help Americans instead of Africans and then offered this advice: "The U.S. economy is slowing down and is obviously in a recession. If you keep on funneling your money outside of your own country during an economic crisis, there will come a time that you will have nothing for others and for yourselves." Others mildly accused us of being self-aggrandizing by agreeing to the interviews.

I used to think that the world's most venal people spent their time calling talk radio. But the anonymity and ease of the Web seems to spawn an unusually poisonous venom. Because the NBC and CNN sites both had links back to Joseph's YouTube video, that one seemed to draw the harshest fire.

Joan and I read our laptop silently, each of us trying to absorb why people seemed so angry. Meanwhile, Hannah and Joseph continued to take turns broadcasting comments aloud. "Oh, this is a good one. Listen," Joseph announced. "PaintballSlave writes: 'That girl is an idiot. The guy in the Mercedes probably went to college, worked his ass off, got a good job, and kept working hard to buy that fancy car. While the homeless guy sits on his ass. Should they be equal? You a communist or something?'" The kids cackled over that one.

Hannah followed by reciting the post of Angrydrunkdwarf, who appeared to live up to his name: "This is what you might expect from someone who has been given a lot, yet has never worked a day in her life. You see raw idealistic immaturity. She has no real concept of money, yet knows what's best in how others should use it."

After each one, they searched through the remarks for something juicier. Maybe it's the ubiquity of the Internet in their lives or the casualness of commenting over the Web, but teenagers don't seem flustered by the hostility of others online. Each nastygram was a source of amusement, a morsel to be savored at full volume.

Our kids might have been having a good time in Room 102, but over in Room 101, Joan didn't think any of this was very funny. Months earlier she had balked about permitting the media to do stories. Now our family was in the crosshairs of snipers firing verbal tomatoes. I could feel her tense up, the layering bricks of anger and anxiety building. Since I had done my work in public as a journalist for decades and was accustomed to the occasional malevolent note, I wasn't quite as upset. But I also recognized that these criticisms were more personal, aimed more directly at us. Joan's protectiveness wasn't unreasonable.

Then Rooms 101 and 102 collided hard. As Joan scanned the screen, her eyes grew big, and she quickly and silently tapped the laptop screen with her index finger, guiding me to a comment our kids hadn't read yet by some creature calling him- or herself RealRabbiShmuley. "Fucking SPOILED WHORE who knows NOTHING. The whore needs to be dropped off in downtown Detroit to experience some REAL diversity. Just fucking be raped by a negro allready [sic] and DIE!"

The game had shifted from benign to shocking. Joan's eyes welled with tears, her face reflecting her horror at those hurtful words, the idea that someone might suggest that her daughter be raped. In a flood of emotion, she even worried that Hannah and Joseph might feel less committed to our project in the face of such vitriolic public criticism. *The kids should not read that. Let's cut off the Internet time right now,* she whispered urgently to me. Sitting on that bed, Joan was no longer a philanthropist or a visitor fascinated by African history. She was a mother, primal, instinctive, and intense.

I never got a chance to respond to her demand. From

211

the other room, Hannah howled in a stream of amazement, "OhmyGodlookatthisit'sincrediblelisten."

She had read only the first few words aloud—"Fucking SPOILED WHORE who"—when Joan shouted her down. "No, no, no, Han, I do not want to hear that."

"Oh, c'mon, Mom," Hannah protested, with a small laugh. "You gotta give the guy credit—at least he's creative. Raped by a Negro already and die."

"Hannah, shut up. I do not want to hear another word of that crap. Not. Another. Word," Joan thundered, snapping shut the laptop in the adults' room with an aggressive flick. "I'm going to dinner, and you should too."

Hannah, Joseph, and I glanced at one another silently. Clearly Joan's dinner command was not a request or a suggestion. We quickly slipped on our shoes and followed her outside to the dining room.

The change of venue did us all some good. Later that night we more calmly totaled up positive comments versus negative ones. The result: two to one in favor of our project. I guess that was tolerable, because emotions remained calm until we got home to Atlanta.

The night before we headed home, back in Accra, we shared one more evening of chicken fights. Hannah demonstrated synchronized swimming moves she had seen on the Ghanaian TV networks and did fairly decent handstands in the pool as Joseph and Joan danced around her, flapping their arms and hands with broad frozen beauty-pageant smiles.

At dinner Hannah led a short game of "Would You Rather . . . ," asking us to choose between a pair of horrible choices. "Would you rather always have to say what's on your mind or never be able to speak again?" "Would you rather lose your arms or lose your legs?" "Would you rather be the circus person who has knives thrown at him or the one who puts his head into the lion?"

We played; we laughed. When the kids asked for seconds on chocolate tarts for their farewell meal, Joan quickly said yes. We were relaxed. We were happy. We had shared, given, and learned.

As the kids consumed dessert (in about the same amount of time it takes to read this sentence), Joan unveiled her last assignment of the trip. She pulled from her bag a sheet of clear stickers and began to peel them off and distribute them. The handwritten questions were to be glued to corners of our personal journal pages.

"Okay, here's the first question: what was your contribution to fighting hunger in Africa last week?" We took the stickers, placed them neatly in our journals, paused for a minute or so to think, and then began scribbling. Hannah and Joan wrote about meeting people, letting them know that we had come thousands of miles because we cared about their progress. They described the encouragement we provided, both to the villagers and to Hunger Project staffers, each group eager for affirmation that they were winning the fight against poverty in their part of the world.

Listening to them read their answers, I thought about American parents' focus on their children's self-esteem. Book after book urges mothers and fathers to help their kids believe in their abilities, so they'll have greater success and

213

be able to sidestep the evils of copycatting or withdrawal. We would never dream of missing our kids' shows or sports events, cheering their effort after strikeouts or their energy in badly sung musical notes. Schools share in the recognition of the need for self-esteem, issuing awards and trophies by the dozens, if not hundreds. The result is that we have created either the most self-confident or the most self-absorbed people on earth.

If only the villagers we had met in Ghana could have some of that mojo. But that kind of affirmation is hard to find at the end of a dirt road. Hannah and Joan recognized that, understanding how important our offer of support could be.

After a few minutes, Joan doled out the second set of stickers. This one asked, "Who would you like to get to know better? Why?" More thinking, more writing. Joseph filled three pages of his journal with multisentence descriptions of a dozen people, including Jacob Assan, the disheveled farmer in Dome who had inadvertently triggered the photo panic; Hannah listed thirty folks she had met, including "the hot waiter" she had ogled at the Jofel Restaurant in Kumasi.

With her final sticker, Joan fired directly for the bull's-eye. "How do you think our family project is going? (Use specific examples of things that feel right and things you wish were different.)" It was such a simple question that it might have been easy to give the rote answer that kids always toss out when parents ask, "How was school today?"—"Good."

Hannah, the caring soul, offered that "the project is going very well. We are giving them hope." Joseph focused on the villagers' future prospects as well as our education. His simple sentence: "We learned the people were not hungry, but they needed opportunity." Joan also mentioned hope and support, but her journal entry quickly turned to our family dynamic. "Kevin and I have more opps to support our kids' development with these increased and deeper interactions (purposeful living). And H+J have been getting along well, and they are creating memories to last a lifetime. They are engaged and committed to the project."

I needed more time. And then even more time. My journal entry spanned four pages. My mind flooded with scenes from the Atlanta Diner, from our dining room table, from meetings and house-purging days. Time spent together learning, debating, voting, and laughing. We had studied the root causes of hunger and poverty at the right hand of Joan Holmes and John Coonrod. We had wrestled with what we could do to help, and then wrestled some more. "The concept is somewhat counterintuitive," I wrote in my journal. "The more you help doesn't translate into more activity on your behalf. People must help themselves be self-reliant. This trip was illuminating from that perspective, to see the joy and sense of achievement on the faces of the people living an hour's drive from a main road; to watch them perform in skits designed to educate themselves; to see the communities come together."

With that last phrase, I paused in my writing. As I looked around the table, I realized how much *our* community of four had come together. From the decision to sell our house to the travel to Ghana's rural villages and all of our activities in between, the power of half was deepening relationships in our family.

To put it in a literary context, we had come of age. We had coalesced as a family, brought together by a mission that really mattered. Maybe it was a bit premature to claim victory, but sitting there at the dinner table in Accra, Ghana, I believed we had found our family legend. We knew what we wanted to stand for.

The return to Atlanta brought us a cold dose of reality. A year and a half after we had put our home on the market, it remained unsold. Sally kept plugging away, holding open houses and placing ads, but the buyers had dried up with the recession in full bite. Sally sent an occasional e-mail update ("We had 7 at the Open House; none qualify"); I could barely stomach reading them.

Each month we paid two bills for heat, water, power, garbage collection, insurance, and the rest. The upstairs air-conditioning compressor died at the old house, so we shelled out two thousand dollars to repair it. Bowing to market conditions, we dropped our asking price a couple more times, but that didn't boost traffic either. We were the stalled car on the side of the road, the boat dead in the water. We discussed leasing the house, even turning it into a bed-and-breakfast. A friend recommended that we sell the Walker Terrace house and move back to our larger place. But we knew why we were selling, so we just hunkered down and waited. As the real estate agents always say, "It only takes one."

The pain was compounded by our pledge to the Hunger Project. The first $80,000 had come due, money we had expected to harvest from the house sale long before we needed to write a donation check. Suddenly we had to figure out what to do.

In the old days, before we had empowered the kids as equal partners on this project, Joan and I would have sorted our options and then made the decision. But that was then. For the past year we had discussed and voted with equal shares. We had been a democracy through all the fun stuff, deciding who would get our money. Now it was tough-choice time, and Joan and I recognized that Hannah and Joseph needed to be players in deciding on a strategy.

So, one evening a few days after we returned from Ghana, we gathered in the living room of the Walker Terrace house. Hannah and Joan sat on the sofa while Joseph and I took armchairs. Joan took a sip of water, then began.

"You guys know that we have a commitment to the Hunger Project and we owe them eighty thousand dollars. You also know that we haven't sold the house."

"Yeah, tell me about it," Joseph said.

Joan ignored his response and plowed ahead. "As result, we need to make some decisions. From what I can see, there really are only three choices. First, we can tell the Hunger Project that we haven't sold the house and that they need to wait until we do. In other words, push back our project's start date. Second, we can pay them a little bit, maybe a few thousand dollars, and tell them the rest is coming later. Hopefully, it won't be long. Or third, we can use other funds we have in savings. Now, Han, you need to know that that's your college money."

A year ago I would have blurted the answer. I would have told everyone how fiscally irresponsible it would be to use college savings money. I would have explained to Hannah how it might limit her choice of schools. I would have set down the rules. But under the structure of our power-balanced project, I decided to wait for others to offer their thoughts first.

Come to think of it, I'm not sure I could have gotten the first word in anyway. Hannah was that quick. "That's a no-brainer. Nothing has changed in Africa. Not one thing," she exclaimed, her thoughts circling to the need for buildings like the corn mill and the school. "Those people need us as much as they did before. We should definitely use our savings, and we'll repay the college fund somehow. Or I'll figure out something for college. Let's keep our promise."

She leaned forward on the couch, listening eagerly for agreement or dissent. From the brown patterned armchair across the room, Joseph, the former skeptic, felt his thoughts going to Jacob Assan, the farmer. Then he added his vote. "I definitely agree. We committed to this."

I looked at Joan, who smiled and addressed the kids. "That's kind of what I thought you might say. But you guys do realize how serious this might be, right? We have no idea what price we will eventually get for our house."

"Yeah, we get it, Mom," Hannah shot back, more out of

impatience than annoyance. "But I have no idea why we're even addressing it. We made a commitment. We keep it."

Later that evening I circled back around to our various pools of money, checking the status of our bank and investment accounts. The rules of the game seemed to have shifted so much since we had decided to take on this project. It was supposed to be half a house for us and half a house for charity, with funds used when they came in. Now, with home prices plunging, we weren't going to clear half. And the timing was serious cart-before-the-horse material.

Still, we had some undesignated funds in our accounts. We also knew that our newly reduced lifestyle would call for less feeding and watering (once the other house sold). Most important, we had leadership from our kids. Joan had explained the potential consequences of making the payments, and Hannah and Joseph had made informed choices. Somehow, we felt, those decisions needed to be respected.

Beyond that, the kids were right: we had made a commitment. From the time they were young, our kids learned to keep promises. In matters big and small, we kept our word, even when it was uncomfortable or situations changed. To renege on a vow this central to our lives would be a huge error in parenting.

Two days later I sent money to the Hunger Project.

In the past, when our family had returned from a ski trip or other vacation, I had noticed that the holiday mode evaporated incredibly quickly. Relaxation melted away, real life crept in, stresses mounted. Interpersonally, the goodwill among family members faded into a more distant every-man-for-himself operation. More than once after trips, I'd asked Joan, "Did we even go somewhere?"

But our journey to Ghana had been so much more than a vacation, and when the school year began in late August, I began to notice small signs of lasting change in our family. After all, transformation is filled with baby steps, not quantum leaps.

Hannah's leadership blossomed, for one thing. She ran for Atlanta Girls' School's Circle of Sisters, the student council, and won for the second straight year. Then she was voted cocaptain of AGS varsity volleyball by her teammates, a decision later overturned by the AGS athletic director because Hannah was only a sophomore and the AD wanted a junior to step up. I watched carefully as Hannah reacted to the news of her demotion, but she just shrugged and said confidently, "I think I have a good chance next year or the year after." Then she praised the other girl.

Soon after, Hannah turned sixteen, and to celebrate she and I signed up to work on a Habitat house. For insurance reasons, Habitat doesn't allow workers under the age of sixteen, so Hannah had served food and visited the work sites but had never actually picked up a paintbrush or a hammer. Now that she was of age, we rose mighty early for a Saturday (especially for a teenager), and Hannah spent the day cutting siding with me and caulking alongside the exuberant soon-to-be homeowner, Freda Parker. When Hannah wasn't working, she was texting her friends about how much fun she was having. "Now all my friends can't wait until they're sixteen so they can build too," she told me as we drove home.

Hannah decided to test-drive other service opportunities too, this time with the rest of our family in the mix. She pushed us until we agreed to starve our way through the 30 Hour Famine, a day-plus fast encouraged by the nonprofit group World Vision. When Joseph balked, she prodded, "C'mon, dude, it will help us understand what it feels like to be hungry." (After a hungry stretch in the first eight hours, we felt far fewer pangs than we had expected.) Another time, she and Joan went to the American Red Cross to donate blood, but they were turned away because they had visited a malaria zone within the past twelve months. When they returned home, Joan announced with a chuckle that "Hannah and I were rejected from community service because of our community service."

Hannah's values became evident in other ways too. One day she and I were riding in the Toaster, her fingers seemingly incapable of not pressing radio buttons. As with the iPod we had shared in Ghana, Hannah was in control of the music, and she was exercising her authority. The classic rock station was playing the Eagles' "Take It Easy" for about the ten thousandth time. Next. Her favorite hip-hop channel was taking a commercial break. Next. The light rock station rolled out an oldie that triggered "Oh my God, how boring." Next. The Top 40 station, Star94, was playing "Kiss Kiss," a song by R & B singer Chris Brown. Hannah let it play.

"I like him—he's got a great voice," I said while Brown sang, "They hatin' on me . . . they wanna diss, diss . . ."

From the same passenger seat from which she had seen the homeless man and the Mercedes, Hannah surprised me again. "He may have a great voice, but you'd hate him if you knew more about him, Dad. He's gross. He's got like twenty-one cars, all this ridiculous excess with Lamborghinis and Porsches, and this stupid massive house. Yuck." I just smiled. I had no problem being set straight by my daughter.

Meanwhile, Joan and I noticed signs of leadership emerging in Joseph, who had turned fourteen. Back in seventh grade, he had wanted to form a band for the school talent show. He thought he had his drummer, singer, and bassist lined up to join his guitar playing. But the group fell apart days before the audition, and when the show date came, Joseph found himself in the audience watching a bunch of his friends perform. He wasn't about to let that happen again. In eighth grade, he held tryouts and texted his band mates to make sure they would show up for rehearsals. Their band, which he named Delusional, led off the show.

On a Wednesday morning before Halloween, the Atlanta paper ran on the front of its Living section one of those insipid articles about how kids eat too much candy at Halloween. I stood in the kitchen skimming the piece, the paper spread out on the black granite countertop. To my right, the Hamilton Beach coffeemaker had entered the gurgling phase just before the end of the drip cycle when Joseph came down to get breakfast. He grabbed some Eggo waffles from the freezer and tossed them into the toaster oven, then glanced over my shoulder at the article. "Hey, Dad, read me their 'Tips for Dealing with the Sugarfest.' Those things are always hilariously stupid."

I put on a fake newscaster voice and began to read the series of painfully obvious suggestions. " 'Sticky candy such as taffy and gummies as well as hard candy like lollipops are particularly bad for your teeth.'"

"Duh," Joseph replied.

"'Beware of braces.'"

"Double duh."

After four or five more, I was really hamming it up, emoting as if I were trying out for *Macbeth*. "'Make sure your goblins don't go to bed without flossing and brushing their teeth.'"

Joseph could barely spit out a reply to that one, his laughter interfering with his speech. "Holy crap, these people think we're total morons. You mean I should brush my teeth before bed after I eat a bunch of candy? Really?"

Finally I got to the last item. Still in Shakespearean performance mode, I proclaimed grandly, "'Talk to your child about ways to repackage the extra candy, such as making gift bags for retirement homes, homeless shelters, or for care packages for military members stationed overseas.'"

Joseph's face quickly morphed from laughter to seriousness. "That's the first good one. I like that idea. We should definitely do something like that." (In the end he only trick-or-treated for about fifteen minutes and ended up with little surplus.)

The biggest shift might have been in Hannah and Joseph's relationship. They sought each other's advice more often, Hannah asking her little brother's help with iMovie or in filming a project for a class in world history.

One day in the car, I griped to her that Joseph was off to a slow start in baseball.

"Is he working at it?" she asked me.

"Not as hard as I think he should," I replied, "but I think he's done listening to me about it."

"I'll talk to him about it," she volunteered, and later that evening she ripped him for being lazy, hitting only a few times a week, and letting his opportunity to be on the West-minster Schools team slip. Our girl was maturing before our eyes. Was it a result of our project or the natural growth of a young woman? I'm not sure I could tell you.

During Christmas break we headed to the west coast of Florida to spend the holidays with Joan's parents. On the Saturday morning after Christmas, I poured a cup of coffee, dropped in a dollop of milk, and scanned the *Wall Street Journal.* On page A9, wedged behind news about the scam-mer Bernard Madoff, was a piece on the Opinion page head-lined "A Conservative Philanthropist Looks to the Future."

The article focused on Bill Simon, the cochair of a large foundation started by his father, the former treasury secre-tary. Simon talked about the tough economic times and the trickle-down impact on nonprofits. Since investors were ex-periencing painful declines in their stock portfolios, "there are only so many places that they can try to cut back. And one of them is their giving." Then Simon said something I'll never forget. "People will not sell their houses to fund char-itable giving."

I shrieked so loudly that it jarred Joan, who immediately looked up from the kitchen. "What—what is it?" she asked, her voice concerned.

"Listen to this, listen to this," I gurgled. By now Joseph had come over, abandoning the SpongeBob SquarePants cartoons he had been watching from the beige living room rug. Hannah opened the bedroom door, bleary-eyed in her oversized T-shirt. "What happened?"

I briefly described who Simon was and set some context about the plunging stock market. Then I paused briefly and read the line aloud: "'People will not sell their houses to fund charitable giving.'"

Hannah, still barely awake, smiled slightly. "We are," she said. Joseph grunted mild approval. But Joan shot back, "He's right, they won't."

"But we are," I protested, echoing Hannah.

"Yes, but c'mon, Kev, you *know* that selling the house was never the point. Our home was just a tool, a mechanism for us to rally as a unit to make a little difference in the world."

I stopped dead in my tracks. Joan was right. I had been so surprised by Simon's use of the house example that I had lost sight of what I had known all along: we had always called our adventure "the family project," because first and foremost it was about our family. It was enlightened self-interest. The Secret Sauce to family togetherness was being out in the community for others, regardless of how *community* was defined—the neighborhood, the city, the world.

Friends and others who asked us about the whys, wheres, and hows of our project always focused on magnitude and experience: the big house, the big donation, or the trip to Africa. They never appreciated the transformational energy of the process—the worksheets, the debates, the critical power-sharing votes. They never saw the internal workings of a family eager to stand for something collectively, to stop accumulating, to get off the treadmill, to unify around a single purpose.

For us, the American Dream meant, as Joseph said in his movie, "that sharing can lead to a better life for others." That didn't necessarily require a huge sacrifice; it just required figuring out what we could give. We had more than enough house, so we gave up half of that. If we hadn't, we would have given time or talent amounting to half of something else.

And it always made us cringe when others misunderstood and said things like "Oh, you're the folks who are giving away half of everything you own." No, far from it. We were giving away half of one thing: our house. We still took family vacations; we still owned our cars. We just chose one element of our collective lives that we could hand off to someone else and make others' prospects a bit brighter. It didn't mean I couldn't crave a TV or Hannah couldn't go dress shopping or Joan couldn't lust for a trip to Rome. We weren't setting the goal line beyond the house—at least, not yet.

Still, what family wouldn't trade stuff for togetherness? In a world where we often have excess, what would happen if we all chose just one thing in our lives that we have enough of and gave away half? Magic. Think about it: cutting in half the number of weekly lattes, the hours spent online, the excess blood in our bodies.

One trick we learned: sustained giving is more unifying. We lived it over time. For us, arriving home each day to a more modest home has been a steady, visible reminder of our shared purpose. As a result, giving away half the clothes in the closet might be good, while a regular monthly lemonade and espresso stand might be even better.

Beyond that, we discovered that finding the right way to serve is a bit harder than it looks. I wish it were as easy as "just do it." While this is far from a complete list, some questions we realized we needed to ask include

- Will our work empower or be a Band-Aid? The latter is fine for relief work but will undoubtedly fail in creating long-term change.
- Do we respect the culture? This applies locally or globally. Another way to ask is, Do we have enough humility to see our new partners (that is, the recipients) as equals?
- Are those partners fully engaged in designing the project? The key word in there is *fully*. If not, I can almost guarantee a flop.
- Are we doing this work for the same reasons as our partners, the folks we're trying to help? Or do we have a different agenda?
- Are we committed for the long haul? Real change never happens overnight.

You may find different queries more relevant for work with young children, the environment, or animal rescue, but we found that these are helpful not only for overseas development but for substance abuse, poverty, homelessness, and at-risk youth, among others.

I looked around that breakfast room in Florida, with the sun streaming in over Sarasota Bay, Hannah in her volleyball tournament shirt, Joseph's hair a mess, Joan in her green patterned pajamas, and me a little sweaty from a morning run: a family, just like millions of others.

From day one, Hannah had wanted to change the world. It took a while, but Joseph joined in. And Joan and I wanted to create a New New Normal for ourselves. Or maybe it was just *normal* with a lowercase *n*. Either way, I must say, it was a darn good place to live.

We sat down for breakfast together.

HANNAH'S TAKE

Dealing with Setbacks

NO MATTER WHAT PROJECT YOU DO, YOU'RE ALMOST GUARANTEED to have setbacks, major or minor. I think lots of us have had a volunteer experience where we haven't felt appreciated. Throughout my family's project, we had both major and minor setbacks. Some small ones included problems securing our Ghanaian visas and the pain of all the shots we had to get. The major stumble, of course, was the difficulty selling our house. The bummer economy could not have arrived at a worse time, and our house sat on the market for more than two years. We needed the money from the sale to make our pledge to the Hunger Project, and we had to scramble to find a way to pay without it.

But as Henry Ford once said, "Failure is only the opportunity to begin again more intelligently." Because the biggest of our setbacks were financial, I interviewed my mom on the best way to cope with some common roadblocks. "While you're adjusting to the situation, you have to think about what it is you're trying to accomplish with your project," she told me. "You have to ask yourself two questions: Is this inconvenience worth losing the project? Or does it in fact make it richer? In other words, does having to struggle and learn from it make it more yours?" In our case, I would say that not being able to sell the house helped us feel the project more deeply and forced us to think many times about what we were doing and why.

Although your problems may involve issues with money or some other unspoken topic, parents need to keep kids informed. Keeping them in the loop about the things that are going wrong will make the project seem more real to them. After a year of not being able to sell our house, our first payment to the Hunger Project was due. We sat down as a family and discussed whether we should take money out of Joseph's and my college funds or tell the Hunger Project that we just couldn't get the money. We adapted to the situation we were given and decided as a family to take money out of the college funds. No matter what the setback, there is a solution.

Epilogue

The dream was always running ahead of me.
To catch up, to live for a moment in unison with it,
that was the miracle.

— Anaïs Nin

'M NOT GREAT at predicting the future. But here's what I can tell you: The villagers in Hunger Project–empowered communities in Ghana will become healthier, better educated, and more self-sufficient. Infant mortality will drop; I know, because not a single baby or mother has died in an epicenter health clinic in Ghana. Not one. And more students, especially girls, will go to secondary school; as the gender equality programs train more parents to view their children more evenly, girls begin to get their fair share. Successful businesses will be built too, if the past is any guide; the epicenters' microfinance programs are expanding their lending by hundreds of thousands of dollars a year, mostly by women to women.

Over the next five years, we will continue to fund the development and empowerment of two clusters of villages.

Our relationship with Ghana will last at least until Hannah and Joseph finish high school and begin college. After that, our kids will be on their own, creating their own futures of giving. Like every parent out there, we will have done what we could; in our case, we hope we have nurtured citizens, not consumers. And in our case it was Hannah who helped Joan and me find the right path.

On an April day in 2009, Hannah was driving our eight-year-old Ford Ranger home from her friend Alex's house. She had gotten her driver's license a few weeks earlier, but she needed our permission to borrow any vehicle. We tussled often about whether the truck, which Joan and I had mothballed for two years, was "my truck," as Hannah called it, or "our truck," as Joan and I insisted. In a bid to claim her turf, Hannah hung a smelly pink breast-cancer ribbon air freshener from the rearview mirror.

Now she was driving alone down the Buford Highway Connector, the same road where she and I had first encountered the homeless man two years earlier. This time Hannah decided not to go all the way to the Spring Street intersection, but chose instead to exit earlier, at Monroe Drive. She would take the streets from there.

As she waited behind ten other vehicles for the red light to change, a man walked along the line of cars that idled ahead of her. His clothing was torn. He was filthy. As Hannah told me that night, "The guy was asking for food, and people were rolling up their windows, avoiding him. I was searching around the truck for a Balance bar or something, but I didn't have anything."

The light turned green, and Hannah made a split-second decision. She changed lanes, shifting to the right, and pulled into a Shell station at the bottom of the ramp. Inside the Food Mart, she rounded up a small box of saltines and five Nature Valley granola bars. Total cost: seven dollars. She drove back toward the intersection.

"Excuse me, sir," she yelled, holding the bag out the window. "Would you like some food?"

The man ran to the car. "Thank you very much," he said. As he was walking away, he ripped open the saltines box and began to eat.

From the truck, Hannah knew that all she had done was provide short-term comfort without long-term opportunity. She had learned all of that in the past couple of years, but she still longed to help. So she did. "I don't think that I solved anything," she told us at dinner. "I gave him relief, and hopefully somebody else can take the time to help him get more help."

Maybe he was a project for another family.

A week later our real estate agent, Sally George, called. "I think we're going to get an offer on the house," she told me.

I really didn't know how to feel about that. As the recession had deepened during the fall and winter, home sales had stopped dead—that is, unless you wanted to count the string of foreclosures that triggered transactions at pennies on the dollar. "There just aren't buyers out there," Sally had told us more than once. One day as I was driving, Clark Howard, the syndicated consumer adviser, announced gloomily on his radio show that the nation had a twelve-year supply of homes to absorb; little beyond population growth could take care of that, he predicted. I jabbed the Off button on the radio.

Through another long winter of no sales, Joan and I rarely talked about the house. It was the kind of topic over which our optimistic natures became tied in knots; other than lowering the price, there simply wasn't a whole lot we could do. Occasionally, on a morning walk with the dogs, Joan would burst out in frustration: "What the hell are we going to do about that house, Kev?" My answers offered scant comfort. Sometimes I didn't even try; she just needed to vent.

We did what all needy sellers with an extra home do: we cut the price some more. Now we were down a total of $400,000 from the value at which it had been appraised in 2007. Trading our enormous house for one that better fit our dream had seemed so simple at the outset, but it had turned complicated. Despite Hannah's belief that we would pay back our savings account and still fund our $800,000 commitment to the Hunger Project, any transaction at this price was going to leave us short. We would have to find the funds somewhere else.

In her phone call, Sally had an unusual request. "I think this is the type of buyer who would like to meet you and Joan. Can I set something up for Saturday morning over at the Peachtree Circle house? That way, you can walk them through the home and show them what's what."

Her strategy got us most of the way there. After a week-long series of conversations between the buyer and me (with no agents involved), we had the outline of a contract. Like many real estate deals, this one had its share of messy spots and disputes, emotion and gamesmanship. Sally was annoyed that I agreed to an offer $125,000 lower than our already slashed asking price, but we had no other interested parties anywhere on the horizon. In short, Joan and I felt we were out of options. We had to make this deal work.

After the basic structure had been hammered out, though, we were haggling again, seemingly for the hundredth time with these buyers. Every step of the way felt tenuous.

But we had an edge to make the deal work. We had Rosie.

Just after eleven on Thursday morning, our cleaning team, Hector and Rosie, came into the Walker Terrace house. As they walked through the front door, much to the excitement of the dogs, Hector offered his standard "Hello, Mr. Kevin." I sat at the head of the dining room table, my laptop propped open.

We chatted for a moment or so, and then Hector walked through the kitchen, up the steps, and into the back of the house. But Rosie put down her bags and stood in the kitchen looking at me. Her eyes went to the contract sitting at my right hand; she recognized the form.

"Mr. Kevin, how is the other house?"

"I don't know, Rosie. We're very close to a contract on it. But I'm really not sure it's going to go through. The deal has been very tough. I'm kind of betting against it."

My pessimism clearly caught Rosie's attention. In the past, she and I had discussed the economy, her and Hector's townhouse in the suburbs, and life in her native Brazil. In Rosie's experience, I was almost always upbeat. But listening to me describe the contract, she detected a shift in my normal attitude. She took three steps toward me, crossed the threshold into the dining room, and looked down at me sitting at the table. Her next sentence was a thunderbolt.

"Mr. Kevin, do you believe in prayer?" she began, her English tinged with a strong Portuguese accent.

"Sure, Rosie, of course I do."

"I ask you this because last week, when I went to clean your other house, Mr. Kevin, I prayed hard to God. I asked God to help you sell your house because you want to do good things with the money. I prayed for you."

The cynic in me might have shot back that Joan had buried a statuette of Saint Joseph in our yard two years earlier. A lot of good that did. But I knew better than to mess with this effort. Rosie was praying for us.

Earlier in our family's life, if anyone ever prayed for us, they certainly didn't tell us. I could only imagine what that moment of silence might have sounded like, anyway. "Please, Lord, help the Salwens choose wisely in their next car purchase." Now what we were doing mattered so much that someone had taken time from her own life to ask for divine help for us. As I sat at the table, the thought of that made my eyes well up. Rosie was praying for us.

All I could muster was a meek "Thank you, Rosie. That really means a lot to me. Really."

Later that day Joan came home from school. "I want to talk about something," I said, and I told her the story about Rosie. Then I added, "You know, Joan, I wish this deal were happening at a higher price, but I am totally at peace with it. In fact, if you think about it, every step of the way in this project good things have happened to us. Great people have come into our lives; our kids have blossomed. Good things always seem to happen. I believe they will now too."

The next morning we agreed to the contract.

A bit more than a month later, two years and fifty-nine days after we first put the Peachtree Circle house on the market, we were done. Our one-time Dream House now belonged to someone else.

Our dream had outgrown those walls.

HANNAH'S TAKE

Keeping Track of Your Project

DOCUMENTING IS ONE OF THE MOST IMPORTANT STEPS WHEN doing a family project. Unfortunately, I learned that the hard way during ours.

I never particularly wanted to keep a journal. Even though we were having vital conversations that would seriously affect our project, I figured that since everything was fresh in my mind, I would never forget it. Our French toast dinner at the Atlanta Diner to kick off our decision-making is a perfect example. What would I need that information for? Well, I regret not writing about that night; it made it really difficult for me to remember our conversation later.

Documenting is very helpful for several reasons. First, it makes the story easier to tell and gets every family member on the same page. We found it helped us remember goals, details, and, most important, why we reached certain conclusions. Using her journal, my mom made a PowerPoint presentation in June 2007. It summarized what we had already decided so that we didn't have to go over that stuff again and could pick up right where we left off. This made our meetings more productive (and shorter!). When I began keeping a journal, I made a point of writing down not just the facts but also my feelings during certain parts of our adventure. It became fascinating to see how my perspective changed as I learned more.

Second, documenting helps involve family members who haven't really been engaged. When Joe began to make his movie for the Coldwell Banker "My Home: The American Dream" contest, he became much more passionate about the project. He was inspired to do something that he loves to do, namely, make movies.

There are so many cool new ways to document your personal family project that you just have to find the one that seems best to you. You could make a movie, like we did, or create a newsletter. Apple has a great, easy format to create a photo book that looks like a real coffee-table book for only $29.99 (you can find it on the Apple site, www.apple.com/ilife/iphoto/print-products.html).

One of the great things about working together on a project like this is that every person in your family takes in experiences and information differently. So make sure that you don't have just one "official documenter" and that everyone is writing things down. One family member should be the documenting leader and then divide the jobs, such as photography, scriptwriting, camerawork, and so on.

Documenting as a family helps you relive the successes that you've had with your project. It's a great time to interact with your family about favorite moments. When my family sat down and decided how we were going to document, we reminded each other about chicken fights in the pool in Ghana and unusual foods we saw in Africa (bush meat, anyone?). These offbeat moments help create family history.

Acknowledgments

This book recounts our family's effort to give. But we're amazed at how much people gave *us* as we set about writing it.

The giving began with those who spent countless hours educating us about global poverty. At the Hunger Project, John Coonrod, our travel companion, led the way—and his patience and good humor reflect his optimism about humankind. Hunger Project founder Joan Holmes graciously embraced us, then sat for hours of interviews. When we traveled to Ghana, Dr. Naana mobilized her group led by Isaac, J.S., Janet, Victor, and Little Naana. They made us feel welcome from the first *akwaaba*, but their warmth was dwarfed by their dedication and hard work in making the lives of their countrymen better.

Others gave us the gift of learning how to give: Luana Nissan at the Glenn Institute for Philanthropy and Service Learning taught us about youth philanthropy; Rob Smulian at the Community Foundation for Greater Atlanta educated us about the nuts and bolts of donations; former Colby

College president Bill Cotter graced us with an education about working in Africa; and philanthropy adviser Chip Raymond helped us shape our thinking.

As we decided to write this book, our agents, Amy Hughes and David McCormick, coached and counseled us each step of the way. Our generous "first readers"—George Anders, Michelle Medley, and Grace Lim—forced us to be better, chapter after chapter. Our work was greatly enhanced by their steady stream of challenging questions and thoughtful suggestions.

We offer hearty thank-yous to the team at Houghton Mifflin Harcourt: Bridget Marmion, Lori Glazer, Alia Hanna Habib, Laura Brady, and Carla Gray. Liz Duvall saved our bacon more than we care to admit with her keen copyediting eye. And a deep, deep bow of appreciation goes to our editor, Susan Canavan, who crowbarred the best out of us; this book has her fingerprints all over it (and occasionally shoeprints from a sharp kick or two).

Those who gave us the gift of support and friendship are too numerous to mention. But we'd be remiss not to single out Blair and Lori Schlossberg, Sally George, Amy Unell, Mark Albion, Andrew Brenner, Marc Bortniker, Martin Flaherty, Bruce Boynick, Amy Conlee, and the O'Briens, Sanders, Thompsons, and Phillips. The teams at Atlanta Habitat for Humanity, Atlanta Community Food Bank, and Café 458 inspire us with their compassion and giving. And we learn about community every day from the folks at Atlanta Girls' School and Westminster.

The Wells half of the Salwells (Della, Jere, Judson, and Aubrey) may have scratched their collective head at first, but they were and are our strongest allies. Hannah sends her love to Chelsea Person, Blaise Sullivan, Alex Harrison, and her other close friends for their support and friendship while she wrote this book.

Of course, a book about our family wouldn't be complete without our family. Each step of the way, we felt the love of Val and Andrea Salwen, Bob King, and Steve, Dan, and Tammy. Joan's parents, June and Don King, are as phenomenal as it gets. Alex, Kassy, Liz, and the King clan, as they say here in the South, we love y'all.

Just as we were starting to write this book, Judy Salwen, our mother/grandmother, was hit by a car and killed near her apartment in New York. Two days shy of her eighty-second birthday, Grammy was on her way to a date, another active day in a life lived with energy and passion. A few years ago, she challenged several of us, "Don't honor me when I'm not around. I'd like to be honored while I'm alive." Grammy, we hope we did that, but also know you were with us for every step of this journey.

Finally, no one gave more to this effort than our teammates on this adventure. Joseph, feel free to call us for Pictionary lessons at any time. And Joan, you read each line multiple times, pushed us every step of the way to feel more deeply, and liberally handed out MLs when we needed them most. You two were our toughest and best critics. We feel your love and caring every day.